CHRISTIAN RENEWAL

POTENTIALS
GUIDES FOR PRODUCTIVE LIVING

Wayne E. Oates, General Editor

CHRISTIAN RENEWAL

Living Beyond Burnout

by
CHARLES L. RASSIEUR

THE WESTMINSTER PRESS
Philadelphia

Copyright © 1984 Charles L. Rassieur

All rights reserved—no part of this book may be reproduced in any form without permission in writing from the publisher, except by a reviewer who wishes to quote brief passages in connection with a review in magazine or newspaper.

Scripture quotations from the Revised Standard Version of the Bible are copyrighted 1946, 1952, © 1971, 1973 by the Division of Christian Education of the National Council of the Churches of Christ in the U.S.A., and are used by permission.

Book design by Alice Derr

First edition

Published by The Westminster Press ®
Philadelphia, Pennsylvania

PRINTED IN THE UNITED STATES OF AMERICA
2 4 6 8 9 7 5 3 1

Library of Congress Cataloging in Publication Data

Rassieur, Charles L., 1938–
   Christian renewal.

   (Potentials)
   1. Christian life—Presbyterian authors. 2. Stress (Psychology) 3. Burn out (Psychology) I. Title.
II. Series.
BV4501.2.R33 1984   248.4'851   83-26064
ISBN 0-664-24611-7 (pbk.)

To
the numerous persons over the years who,
by the example
of their vibrant Christian faith and courage,
have shown me it is possible
to be renewed for living
beyond the stress in my own life

Contents

Foreword	9
Preface	13
1. The Sign of the Times	15
2. Your Greatest Asset	30
3. Making All the Ends Meet	45
4. Beyond Easy Answers	67
5. In the Presence of Death	84
6. Your Neighbor as Yourself	101
Questions for Thought and Discussion	*119*

Foreword

The eleven books in this series, Potentials: Guides for Productive Living, speak to your condition and mine in the life we have to live today. The books are designed to ferret out the potentials you have with which to rise above rampant social and psychological problems faced by large numbers of individuals and groups. The purpose of rising above the problems is portrayed as far more than merely your own survival, merely coping, and merely "succeeding" while others fail. These books with one voice encourage you to save your own life by living with commitment to Jesus Christ, and to be a creative servant of the common good as well as your own good.

In this sense, the books are handbooks of ministry with a new emphasis: coupling your own well-being with the well-being of your neighbor. You use the tools of comfort wherewith God comforts you to be a source of strength to those around you. A conscious effort has been made by each author to keep these two dimensions of the second great commandment of our Lord Jesus Christ in harmony with each other.

The two great commandments are summarized in Luke 10:25–28: "And behold, a lawyer stood up to put him to the test, saying, 'Teacher, what shall I do to inherit eternal life?'

He said to him, 'What is written in the law? How do you read?' And he answered, 'You shall love the Lord your God with all your heart, and with all your soul, and with all your strength, and with all your mind; and your neighbor as yourself.' And he said to him, 'You have answered right; do this, and you will live.' "

Underneath the two dimensions of neighbor and self there is also a persistent theme: The only way you can receive such harmony of thought and action is by the intentional re-centering of your life on the sovereignty of God and the rapid rejection of all idols that would enslave you. The theme, then, of this series of books is that these words of Jesus are the master guides both to the realization of your own potentials and to productive living in the nitty-gritty of your day's work.

The books in this series are unique, and each claims your attention separately in several ways.

First, these books address great social issues of our day, but they do so in terms of your own personal involvement in and responses to the problems. For example, the general problem of the public school system, the waste in American consumerism, the health hazards in a lack of rest and vocational burnout, the crippling effects of a defective mental outlook, and the incursion of Eastern mystical traditions into Western Christian activism are all larger-than-life issues. Yet each author translates the problem into the terms of day-to-day living and gives concrete guidelines as to what you can do about the problem.

Second, these books address the undercurrent of helplessness that overwhelming epidemic problems produce in you. The authors visualize you throwing up your hands and saying: "There is nothing *anyone* can do about it." Then they show you that this is not so, and that there are things *you* can do about it.

Third, the authors have all disciplined themselves to stay off their own soapboxes and to limit oratory about how awful the world is. They refuse to stop at gloomy diagnoses of

Foreword

incurable conditions. They go on to deal with your potentials for changing yourself and your world in very specific ways. They do not let you, the reader, off the hook with vague, global utterances and generalized sermons. They energize you with a sense of hope that is generated by basic information, clear decision-making, and new directions taken by you yourself.

Fourth, these books get their basic interpretations and recommendations from a careful plumbing of the depths of the power of faith in God through Jesus Christ. They are not books that leave you with the illusion that you can lift yourself and your world by pulling hard at your own bootstraps. They energize and inspire you through the hope and strength that God in Christ is making available to you through the wisdom of the Bible and the presence of the living Christ in your life. Not even this, though, is presented in a namby-pamby or trite way. You will be surprised with joy at the freshness of the applications of biblical truths which you have looked at so often that you no longer notice their meaning. You will do many "double takes" with reference to your Bible as you read these books. You will find that the Bread of Life is not too holy or too good for human nature's daily food.

Charles Rassieur writes out of his background as an associate director of the North Central Career Development Center in New Brighton, Minnesota, and designated director of the Samaritan Center for Minneapolis and St. Paul. In this volume he frankly challenges the built-in hopelessness of the popular preoccupation with "burnout." He does so on the basis of a careful and detailed description of the stress factors in your life that tend to overcome and "burn" you out, "burn" you up, and "burn" you down. He demonstrates his thorough knowledge of this kind of fatigue with his own personal experience and the wide range of experiences of persons with whom he has conferred as a pastoral counselor of troubled people. He speaks from an extensive range of research and does so in an intimately personal way that makes you feel that he knows you and is your understanding friend.

Charles Rassieur takes the secular idea of burnout and presents vivid and convincing Christian alternatives to the high costs we pay for the fleeting and transitory aims of our lives. He apprises us of our gifts and assets in reclaiming our resources in the Christian faith. He distinguishes between Christian self-care in dealing with stress and self-centeredness. By Christian self-care he means the cultivation of a growing spiritual center for our affections and devotions to Christ, living by grace and not guilt, being able to say no with a clear conscience, and paying reverent attention to the exercise of our bodies and the maintenance of health.

One of the cardinal characteristics of burnout is despair. He affirms that there are no easy answers to despair. Yet he moves beyond answers to emphasize how, in Jesus Christ, God enters our despair and uses the other edge of despair to produce endurance and triumph within tragedy. He speaks of concrete things you and I can do in the face of despair to lay hold of the rich resources of the Christian faith community in such times.

To me, the last two chapters are the essence of the genuinely Christian life beyond burnout. The threat of death is addressed by the power of the resurrection in a clearly original sense of power. Also, Rassieur brings the book to a climactic utterance by his down-to-earth insistence that the petty stresses of life have their greatest resolution when you and I in response to Jesus Christ respond to the needs of others in a broken and hungry world of people—such as the people of Asia, who have 60 percent of the world population and 30 percent of the land area, whereas North America has 8 percent of the population and 16 percent of the land area. He traces much of our stress to spiritual indifference and points to spiritual concern for other people in the name of Jesus Christ as the great source of renewal.

WAYNE E. OATES

Louisville, Kentucky

Preface

The purpose of this book is to affirm the good news of the gospel that there is renewal for persons who are overburdened with stress and burnout. Although many books have been written recently on the subject of stress management, I know of no book that specifically relates the unique resources of the Christian faith to the pressing contemporary crisis of widespread stress and burnout.

I am grateful to Wayne Oates and The Westminster Press for the kind invitation to write this book and the editorial support and recommendations throughout the writing. The opportunity to work on this book has enabled me to arrive at a clearer understanding and conviction about what I believe to be true about the Christian faith and the enormous resources available to all persons through Jesus Christ.

Chapter 1 offers a review of the nature and extent of the stress and burnout most of us deal with daily. Chapter 2 emphasizes the importance of taking care of oneself as a Christian responsibility and opportunity. Chapter 3 examines implications of the Lordship of Jesus Christ for coping with stress and outlines a strategy for renewal so that excessive stress and burnout can be avoided. Chapter 4 focuses on despair as a particular problem accompanying burnout. Chapter 5 discusses the spiritual renewal available to Christians even in the presence of death. Chapter 6 asserts that our attention as Christians not only should be on our own stress and burnout but also must be directed to the stressful needs of all our neighbors in this world.

The quotations and descriptions of various persons contained in this book have been introduced with fictitious names and details so that complete anonymity is protected. I gladly express my deep gratitude to the persons who permitted me to interview them. I also wish to thank Mary Pat Hanauska and Judi Johnson for their special efforts in helping me to interview cancer patients. To all who gave me permission to use materials from their various experiences I am very grateful.

Once again my wife, Ginni, and two sons, Ted and Bill, have been very supportive. I know that without my family's willingness to endure my preoccupation with another writing project, I could not have undertaken this assignment.

The reader will observe that I have purposely not included any lists of books for recommended reading. For those who are interested, I suggest that the various resources I refer to throughout this book be obtained for wider reading on the subjects I have discussed.

I accept responsibility for all that is contained within the pages that follow.

C.L.R.

New Brighton, Minnesota

Chapter 1
The Sign of the Times

> In 1872 the elder Gross defined shock as a "manifestation of the rude unhinging of the machinery of life."
> *Seymour I. Schwartz, editor in chief*
> Principles of Surgery, *4th ed., p. 115*
> *McGraw-Hill Book Co., 1984*

> Hear the good news!
> Who is in a position to condemn? Only Christ, and Christ died for us, Christ rose for us, Christ reigns in power for us. Christ prays for us.
> Anyone in Christ is of the New Creation: old things have passed away. All things are new.
> Friends: Believe the good news of the Gospel.
> *Worship bulletin*
> *Christ Presbyterian Church*
> *Camp Hill, Pa.*
> *Sept. 26, 1982*

Each day I pick up from my front doorstep a carefully edited record of the "rude unhinging of the machinery of life." The newspaper I read daily offers alarming evidence that most of us are trying to survive under inhuman levels of stress. Moreover, I suspect that the news media report only a fraction of the human struggle that drains and exhausts our spiritual resources.

The widespread character and the depth of the stress and spiritual burnout go largely unnoticed because most of us let very few persons ever know how deeply troubled we are. Nearly one hundred fifty years ago Henry David Thoreau made an observation that remains accurate today for both men and women: "The mass of men lead lives of quiet desperation." (Brooks Atkinson, ed., *Walden and Other Writings of Henry David Thoreau,* p. 7; Modern Library, 1937.) Physician Keith Sehnert has recently cited figures that illustrate the alarming dimensions of the stress that Americans in every walk of life are facing today:

 . . . About 25 million Americans have high blood pressure.
 . . . One million persons have heart attacks each year.
 . . . An estimated eight million people have stomach ulcers.
 . . . 12 million Americans are said to be alcoholics.
 . . . More than 230 million prescriptions are filled each year for tranquilizers. (Keith W. Sehnert, *Stress/Unstress,* p. 14; Augsburg Publishing House, 1981)

It is the sign of the times that our generation has become preoccupied with the immense level of stress in our lives and with the commensurate hopelessness of being able effectively to do anything about it. Just the other day a man who knows he will be retiring in five to seven years was expressing his weariness about trying to perform well enough on his job so he will not be laid off before he is ready to retire. Not only is he mentally and spiritually exhausted by the two hours a day he spends commuting back and forth to work, but he says: "I have reached the point where I just cannot do the work I used to do. I do not have the mental and physical capacity I used to have. And I am afraid the boss will decide it would be more cost effective to hire a younger man." That man is under much stress every day to perform beyond his capacity, or he risks being jobless without the retirement benefits he needs for himself and his family.

Being a pastoral counselor I have countless occasions to

hear people struggling to understand and cope with the burnout of their spiritual, psychological, and physical resources. A young woman recently told me of her fear of burnout. She exclaimed: "I am afraid of burnout because it has already happened to me. I literally collapsed to the ground, and I had to be carried to my bed. I slept for twenty-four hours, and it took me a year to recover my strength. I never want that to happen to me again!" Unfortunately, the daily pressures we all live with push many of us to the same breaking point that woman had to face.

Understanding Stress

Though the word "stress" is commonly used in our daily conversation and is widely understood, it has been difficult for researchers to reach agreement on a precise definition of the term. Hans Selye, a pioneer in the study of stress, has explained the biological response of our bodies when demands are made upon us. In his laboratory, Selye discovered that there is a predictable response as an organism adjusts to the stimuli in its environment, whether they be satisfying or exhausting demands. "Good" stress could result from paddling a canoe across a quiet, tranquil lake. Exhausting or "distressing" stress might come from listening to your boss's unrelenting demands for increased performance, or from the beeping horns and the noxious exhaust fumes of city traffic. (Hans Selye, *The Stress of Life,* rev. ed. p. 74; McGraw-Hill Book Co., 1976.) In any event, according to Selye, our bodies attempt to adjust to our environment. The physiological response made by our bodies for readjustment to a new situation is stress; *"stress is the common denominator of all adaptive reactions in the body."* (Selye, *The Stress of Life,* p. 64.)

Technically, researchers like Selye use the word "stress" to refer only to the changes within your body as you make adjustments to your environment. External demands made upon you are defined by Selye as stressors. The inner signals from your body, such as heightened anxiety, illness, aches and pains, communicate to you that you are trying to cope with increased pressures. It is important to remember that the extent of your stress depends on how you perceive the demands of the situation in which you find yourself. For example, one person donating a pint of blood may simply find the procedure a slight inconvenience in the daily schedule involving very little stress, whereas another person may see the same situation as an experience of great tension and discomfort. How you look at the events in your life is the key to how much stress you have to handle.

It is commonplace for me to see people for counseling who fail to recognize the connection between the numerous problems and conflicts they are facing and the various physical discomforts they are experiencing. When you are dealing with a stressful situation, many important parts of your body are affected, including kidneys, adrenals, liver, blood vessels, heart, brain, nerves, thyroid, pituitary, connective tissue, and white blood cells. (Doris C. Sutterley and Gloria F. Donnelly, eds., *Coping with Stress: A Nursing Perspective,* p. 44; Aspen Systems Corp., 1982.) Gastrointestinal ulcers may be important indicators that you are trying to live with too much pressure in your life. Some persons also find that when their resistance to colds and sickness is lowered, it is time to assess the demands that are being made on them physically, psychologically, and spiritually.

Each one of us is very familiar with the daily need to face demands that are greater than what we personally have to offer. This evening as I was working in the kitchen to prepare our supper, I felt my resources being taxed to their limits as I tried to read a recipe book and block out the noise of three persons talking beside me. Then the phone rang just as I was in the midst of turning the chicken over, slicing an onion, and turning the heat down under the rice so that it would not dry out. I also remember well, a number of years ago when our first child had just been born, a phone call I received in the midst of a meeting I was attending at church. On the other end of the line I immediately recognized the strained voice of my wife. She pleaded with me: "I just cannot cope with this crying child any longer. I know you are in the middle of an important meeting, but I need you to come home right now!" At that moment she was experiencing a desperate imbalance between what she had to give and what was being demanded of her. Needless to say, I promptly went home because of the resulting stress her phone call created within me.

But many persons are not making those phone calls to ask for help. Surprisingly, many people underestimate, or choose to deny, the high levels of stress in their lives. Perhaps we have been trained to think that we should be able to handle anything, regardless of how great the shock is to our system. It is commonplace to overhear well-wishers at a funeral comment about the surviving spouse or family member who is managing to maintain a stoic outer shell to cover the deep inner grief, "My, what a strong, faithful person!" We are so often rewarded for giving the appearance of strength under the most trying circumstances that we begin believing, ourselves, that there should be little we cannot handle. Then we fail to take seriously the signals from our bodies and our feelings telling us that we are becoming quite vulnerable to physical illness or emotional upset and instability.

An important spiritual indicator that stress is mounting in our lives is the temptation *to compromise our spiritual and moral values.* When we are not under pressure, most of us are quite faithful to our highest moral and spiritual principles. But the more the sources of stress mount up, the easier we find it to make choices we would have earlier considered unthinkable. We can only guess at the pressures Judas felt when he went to the authorities and told them that for a few pieces of silver he would betray his Lord. And what of Peter? Jesus knew that under pressure Peter would compromise and deny that he ever knew him. And deny Jesus is exactly what Peter did, three times before the cock crowed, just as Jesus had predicted. What are the pressures that persuade many ordinary persons to cheat on their income tax, steal from their employers, shoplift, fail to pay their creditors, and give less than an honest day's work? Invariably, when persons describe how they have been unfaithful to their spouse, they also speak at the same time of numerous other pressures in their work or in their severely conflicted marriage. Even a quickened temper and a failure of patience with one's children can be a spiritual warning that stress is getting out of hand in other areas of one's life. Unquestionably, coping with increased stress often leads to the compromise of spiritual values for the sake of expediency.

Many persons do not realize that increased stress coming from several different sources in one's life can have the cumulative effect of sharply diminishing physical and spiritual resources for coping. Because we often dismiss many sources of stress, saying that they are inconsequential, we may not realize how vulnerable we are becoming to physical and spiritual burnout.

For over thirty years researchers have been studying the relationships between crises in people's lives and the onset and progression of illness. Consistently the data have shown that there is a close connection between daily pressures and the breakdown of healthy bodily functioning. Research findings support the conclusion that if

> it takes too much effort to cope with the environment, we have less to spare for preventing disease. When life is too hectic, and when coping attempts fail, illness is the unhappy result. (Thomas H. Holmes and Minoru Masuda, "Psychosomatic Syndrome," *Psychology Today,* Vol. 5, No. 11, April 1972, p. 106)

The following Social Readjustment Rating Scale offers a numerical approach for estimating the cumulative effect of stress in one's life resulting in greater vulnerability to illness. Typical daily crises are, for the preceding twelve months, ranked in order of the seriousness of the adjustment one must make in order to accommodate such changes. Thomas Holmes explains that the more change you have, the more likely you are to get sick. Of those people with 300 or more Life Change Units for the past year, almost 80 percent get sick in the near future; with 150 to 299 Life Change Units, about 50 percent get sick in the near future; and with less than 150 Life Change Units, only about 30 percent get sick in the near future. So, the higher your Life Change Score, the harder you should work to stay well. (Correspondence with the author, December 14, 1983.)

SOCIAL READJUSTMENT RATING SCALE

Rank	Life Event	Mean Value
1	Death of spouse	100
2	Divorce	73
3	Marital separation	65
4	Detention in jail or other institution	63
5	Death of close family member	63
6	Major personal injury or illness	53
7	Marriage	50
8	Being fired at work	47
9	Marital reconciliation	45
10	Retirement	45
11	Major change in health or behavior of family member	44
12	Pregnancy	40
13	Sexual difficulties	39

Rank	Life Event	Mean Value
14	Gain of new family member	39
15	Major business readjustment	39
16	Major change in financial state	38
17	Death of close friend	37
18	Change to different line of work	36
19	Major change in number of arguments with spouse	35
20	Taking out a mortgage or loan for major purchase	31
21	Foreclosure on a mortgage or loan	30
22	Major change in responsibilities at work	29
23	Son or daughter leaving home	29
24	Trouble with in-laws	29
25	Outstanding personal achievement	28
26	Wife beginning or ceasing work outside the home	26
27	Beginning or ceasing formal schooling	26
28	Change in living conditions	25
29	Revision of personal habits	24
30	Trouble with boss	23
31	Major change in work hours or conditions	20
32	Change in residence	20
33	Change in schools	20
34	Major change in type or amount of recreation	19
35	Major change in church activities	19
36	Major change in social activities	18
37	Taking out a mortgage or loan for lesser purchase	17
38	Major change in sleeping habits	16
39	Major change in number of family get-togethers	15
40	Major change in eating habits	15
41	Vacation	13
42	Christmas	12
43	Minor violations of the law	11

> (Reprinted with permission. An earlier version of this table appeared in Thomas H. Holmes and Richard H. Rahe, "The Social Readjustment Rating Scale," *Journal of Psychosomatic Research,* Vol. 11, pp. 213–218. Copyright 1967, Pergamon Press, Ltd.)

If I want to kid myself about the amount of stress in my life, this list gives me a realistic view of the pressures to which I have to adjust, spiritually, mentally, and physiologically. It is not just the major calamities of life that place great demands upon me, such as the death of a parent or the loss of my job, but also all the hundreds of daily urgencies that clamor for my attention. Of course Selye was right with his observation that "complete freedom from stress is death." (Hans Selye, *Stress Without Distress,* p. 20; New American Library, 1975.) Indeed, lest we forget, the apostle Paul reminds us by his own example that the Christian is called to a life of risk, pressure, and stress:

> Five times I have received at the hands of the Jews the forty lashes less one. Three times I have been beaten with rods; once I was stoned. Three times I have been shipwrecked; a night and a day I have been adrift at sea; on frequent journeys, in danger from rivers, danger from robbers, danger from my own people, danger from Gentiles, danger in the city, danger in the wilderness, danger at sea, danger from false brethren; in toil and hardship, through many a sleepless night, in hunger and thirst, often without food, in cold and exposure. And, apart from other things, there is the daily pressure upon me of my anxiety for all the churches. (II Cor. 11:24–28)

Stress is surely the sign of our time and certainly an inescapable reality for any who would share the Christian faith with Paul.

Stress Plus Stress Equals Burnout

Stress is a fact of life. The Christian life involves stress, sometimes great amounts of it, as well as joy, renewal, and hope. But in many people's lives, stress has gotten out of hand and the result has been what is called burnout. The following true account of a thirty-eight-year-old physician could apply to many other persons on their way to becoming physically and spiritually exhausted.

> He was now working on Saturdays and Sundays. During the past year he had scheduled a vacation with his family which he had cancelled, using the time to complete paperwork that had accumulated .... Both at work and at home he had become increasingly moody and irritable, and he had frequent outbursts of temper....
> "I've been spending eight hours a day at work," he said, "but I seem to be getting further behind." He would take volumes of work home and stay up half the night trying to complete it. He had become increasingly anxious and noted that both his clinical care of patients and his medical judgement had deteriorated. Because of this, he felt that the nursing staff held him in contempt.
> His wife commented that a similar pattern had occurred shortly before he had left each of his previous jobs. The doctor reported that his sleep had become poor, with frequent awakenings, and that he lost 18 pounds during the preceding 10 weeks. He had begun to use tranquilizing drugs on a daily basis and to drink liquor in order to achieve sleep. (This is a case described by Richard C. W. Hall, Earl R. Gardner, Mark Perl, Sondra K. Stickney, and Betty Pfefferbaum, "The Professional Burnout Syndrome," *Psychiatric Opinion*, Vol. 16, No. 4, April 1979, pp. 13–16.)

The Sign of the Times

I recently ran across this entry in a dictionary: "*to burn out; to burn till the fuel is exhausted, and the fire ceases.*" (*Webster's New Twentieth Century Dictionary of the English Language,* p. 244; World Publishing Co., 1971.) This definition describes very well what had happened to the doctor. All his coping resources had ceased to function adequately.

Herbert J. Freudenberger is a psychologist who has pioneered in studying and writing about burnout. Trying to explain what he had observed in himself and others working in human service agencies, he was helped by the following dictionary definition of burnout: "to fail, wear out, or become exhausted by making excessive demands on energy, strength, or resources." (Herbert J. Freudenberger, "The Staff Burn-Out Syndrome in Alternative Institutions," *Psychotherapy: Theory, Research and Practice,* Vol. 12, No. 1, Spring 1975, p. 73.) Writing in his book on burnout, Freudenberger clearly identifies burnout as the sign of our time when personal achievement has become an obsession with so many of us. Asserting that burnout is "a demon born of the society and times we live in and our ongoing struggle to invest our lives with meaning" (Herbert J. Freudenberger and Geraldine Richelson, *Burn-out: The High Cost of High Achievement,* p. 2; Bantam Books, 1981), he adds that burnout results from devotion to a cause, a way of life, or relationships that have ended in disillusionment and frustrated hopes (p. 13). Burnout happens in many instances, he explains, because

> we're finding, as Alice did in *Through the Looking-Glass,* that "it takes all the running you can do to keep in the same place. If you want to get somewhere else, you must run at least twice as fast as that." (Freudenberger and Richelson, *Burn-out: The High Cost of Achievement,* p. 4)

Freudenberger suggests the following honest review of one's past six months for estimating roughly how near one is approaching to burnout. Take a careful look at any significant changes in your life, including changes in important interpersonal relationships at home, in the office, or in your social life. Then answer the following questions by using a number from one (for no or little change) to five (for much change) to indicate the amount of change you recognize.

1. Do you tire more easily? Feel fatigued rather than energetic?
2. Are people annoying you by telling you, "You don't look so good lately"?
3. Are you working harder and harder and accomplishing less and less?
4. Are you increasingly cynical and disenchanted?
5. Are you often invaded by a sadness you can't explain?
6. Are you forgetting (appointments, deadlines, personal possessions)?
7. Are you increasingly irritable? More short-tempered? More disappointed in the people around you?
8. Are you seeing close friends and family members less frequently?
9. Are you too busy to do routine things like make phone calls or read reports or send out your Christmas cards?
10. Are you suffering from physical complaints (aches, pains, headaches, a lingering cold)?
11. Do you feel disoriented when the activity of the day comes to a halt?
12. Is joy elusive?
13. Are you unable to laugh at a joke about yourself?
14. Does sex seem like more trouble than it's worth?
15. Do you have very little to say to people?

Now compare your score with the following scale:

0–25 .... You're doing fine.
26–35 .... There are things you should be watching.
36–50 .... You're a candidate for burnout.
51–65 .... You are burning out!
Over 65 .... You're in a dangerous place, threatening to your physical and mental well-being (Freudenberger and Richelson, *Burn-out: The High Cost of Achievement,* pp. 17–19)

If you have a high score, remember that this brief test offers only an approximate indication of the level of stress and burnout in your life. However, take seriously a high score as a warning that it may be time to make significant changes in your attitudes and your life-style.

The urgency for all of us about our vulnerability to burnout is that it is much more pervasive and insidious than the short-term fatigue that is solved by a half-hour nap. Burnout is the exhaustion of the whole person, affecting deeply at least five different areas of one's life. A person's *physical well-being* soon shows the toll of burnout. A prominent symptom of burnout is a general, all-around tiredness that affects one's work and one's homelife.

Intellectual functioning loses its former sharpness when burnout is overtaking a person. That person does not engage in problem-solving with the effectiveness and confidence characteristic of earlier years. *Emotionally,* a person becomes blunted as all one's emotional energy is directed totally into one's work. No emotional liveliness is left over for family relationships or for activities and interests beyond one's work that offer the possibility for creativity and renewal.

Socially, the person who is burned out has a virtually nonexistent support network of caring persons. When I ask such persons how many friends they have with whom they could have discussed their concerns or problems, predictably they sadly indicate with a shake of the head that there are no such friends. Also, the *spiritual* dimension of a person's life is deeply affected by burnout. The meaning for life is lost as one's moral values, sense of hope, and courage for taking risks are eroded by apathy, despair, and cynicism. (These five areas are discussed by I. David Welch, Donald C. Medeiros, and George A. Tate, *Beyond Burnout: How to Enjoy Your Job Again When You've Just About Had Enough,* pp. 6–8; Prentice-Hall, 1982.)

A Spiritual Problem

Burnout is not a new problem. Although we have managed to add some modern refinements to the problem of burnout, we can hardly take credit for inventing it. Burnout is really a condition of the human heart when, in spite of ourselves and for whatever reasons, we stop functioning at our loving, faithful best. Sometimes it is called sin. Often, in the Bible, it is experienced as falling short of God's purpose or, worse yet, being separated from the presence of God.

Burnout is often reflected in the searching question "How long, O Lord, how long must I endure?" The psalmist knows that question well.

> How long, O LORD? Wilt thou forget me for ever?
> How long wilt thou hide thy face from me?
> How long must I bear pain in my soul,
>   and have sorrow in my heart all the day?
> How long shall my enemy be exalted over me?
>   (Ps. 13:1–2)

I have heard that question "How long?" from many persons in troubled marriages. "How long must I endure, wait, hope against hope?" I have also heard that question from parents whose child was going through chemical dependency treatment. "How long, Lord, must I put up with the lies, the deceit, the pain, the ridicule from my child?" The same question of "How long?" arises, too, when one is in an intolerable work situation, or one's income and financial resources are severely limited for months, even years. The psalmist knew well the human cry of burnout: "How long must thy servant endure?" (Ps. 119:84).

Besides the psalmist's sensitivity to the human despair resulting in burnout, the Scriptures offer numerous other examples of emotional and spiritual burnout. The Israelites grew tired and restless when Moses was on Mt. Sinai receiving the Ten Commandments. Out of the despair of moral burnout they demanded that Aaron construct for them a golden calf, sacrificing their spiritual integrity for a god of their own making. And King David's burnout and loss of moral judgment were very evident when he desired Bathsheba and planned for her husband, Uriah, to be killed in battle.

The Scriptures record very accurately the human condition of moral, spiritual, and emotional burnout: One wonders where there can be hope. When researchers such as Hans Selye tell us that we cannot escape the final and total exhaustion of all our resources, the question is inescapable: Where is there hope?

Yet it is precisely in the face of all the burnout in your life and mine, in the face of all human burnout and failure of heart, body, and mind, that a cross is raised so good news can be offered to each one of us. The promise is nothing less than each one of us becoming a New Creation, not a burned-out shell, empty and without purpose or meaning or hope. It is a promise that can be made only by the One who transcends the hopelessness so characteristic of human life today.

The Christian assurance is that we shall live beyond our burnout. The remaining chapters will explore the numerous Christian resources we have for making that promise and assurance a reality within our own lives.

Chapter 2

Your Greatest Asset

And God saw everything that he had made, and behold, it was very good.
Genesis 1:31

Most Americans are in terrible shape. We smoke and drink too much, weigh too much, exercise too little and eat too many of the wrong things.
James F. Fixx
The Complete Book of Running, p. 4
Random House, 1977

Woodstock's assignment is to march guard duty back and forth across the top of Snoopy's doghouse. Snoopy's final words to Woodstock are as urgent as life and death: "... and keep a sharp lookout for the enemy!"

However, Woodstock is so preoccupied with the grave responsibility of his mission that he fails to see the end of the doghouse. Repeatedly, he marches right off the top and lands with a "bonk" on his head.

Snoopy returns to find his dazed and starry-eyed friend trying to pick himself up off the ground. Out of a sense of understanding and compassion, Snoopy offers a new command to Woodstock: "On second thought, keep a sharp lookout for yourself!" (Text from PEANUTS by Charles M. Schulz; © 1982 United Feature Syndicate, Inc. Published in *The Minneapolis Tribune,* Nov. 14, 1982.)

This is the message for this chapter: *You are the greatest asset that God has given you for coping with stress and burnout!* Therefore, look out for yourself so you do not become your own worst enemy. Look out for yourself by taking care of yourself. See to it that you take good care of yourself as the essential prerequisite to being ready for the challenge of stress or the threat of burnout.

The New Priority

Taking care of yourself has not been generally viewed as an essential priority for Christian living. Indeed, giving any thought at all to yourself has been traditionally regarded with suspicion or as inappropriate behavior for a faithful Christian disciple. Jesus made it clear that "whoever would be great among you must be your servant, and whoever would be first among you must be your slave; even as the Son of man came not to be served but to serve" (Matt. 20:26b–28a). Consequently, most of us have learned that we should be quite careful about how we consider ourselves. And lest we forget, we are reminded, "Do nothing from selfishness or conceit, but in humility count others better than yourselves" (Phil. 2:3). And we are to avoid such selfishness because, as the passage continues, Jesus himself emptied himself and took the form of a servant. We even call upon the Holy Spirit to deliver us from preoccupation with ourselves:

> Holy Spirit, love divine,
> Glow within this heart of mine;
> Kindle every high desire;
> Perish self in your pure fire.
> (*The Worshipbook—Services and Hymns,*
> p. 422; Westminster Press, 1972)

In recent years Christians have correctly been critical of the mood in our country which has emphasized the importance of number one. The advertising media seem to have adopted the singular theme of appealing to the importance of "you," your needs, your desires, your fantasies. Such preoccupation with oneself is properly called what it is, narcissism, which is a distorted love of self that is incapable of any genuine interest or care for the needs of others. Indeed, the narcissist has only one person in his or her world, much like the self-centered infant who cries for the world to satisfy all its needs.

It is not difficult to recognize such blatant self-absorption. It was quite evident to me when a young man once asked me to help him find a job where he would make $80,000 to $100,000 a year, because he knew he was so "extraordinary," and "so he could be secure." But the price you always pay for such misguided self-importance is that you are never secure. When you have done it your way and supposedly have everything your way, you still have to have more. There is a bit of such self-centeredness in all of us, and our Christian tradition recognizes it as the effort of each of us to play God. Certainly this characteristic of our human nature is at least part of what Paul has in mind when he reminds us: "For by the grace given to me I bid every one among you not to think of himself more highly than he ought to think" (Rom. 12:3a).

The new priority for Christians is to reclaim the stewardship of their personal resources. In the New Testament, Jesus refers to stewards as those to whom much has been entrusted, which they are to care for prudently according to the will of their master. (See Luke's reference to the faithful and wise steward: Luke 12:41–48.) Each of us has received many personal resources. Those "gifts and graces" include our physical bodies, certain talents and abilities, emotions, the ability to think, and important personal relationships, to name a few. Our perspective is that of the steward who is accountable. And we have been given much for which we are accountable.

Far from irresponsible narcissism, which is the opposite of Christian stewardship, *the new priority is for Christians to practice the stewardship of responsible self-care.* The aim for Christian self-care that manages stress responsibly is *wholeness*. A theologian who has been one of my respected teachers has described Christian wholeness as including "the idea of a strong and healthy body, strong and healthy emotions, a strong and healthy reason, a strong and healthy imagination, and a strong and healthy will, as well as a strong and healthy spirit." (John B. Cobb, Jr., *Theology and Pastoral Care*, p. 28; Fortress Press, 1977.) Having loved ourselves sufficiently to nurture the wholeness of our human experiences and relationships, we then shall be in a much better position to meet the countless demands that are made upon us.

However, many Christians do not give enough attention to their personal wholeness. Perhaps out of concern that they may be too self-centered, such persons frequently invite much unnecessary stress upon themselves because they fail to take care of themselves sufficiently. This failure of essential Christian self-care often occurs in two major areas.

The first common area of frequent stress and burnout is that of interpersonal relationships. Inadequate self-care leads to heightened stress in our relationships with others when clear personal boundaries are not maintained. A normal occurrence in many families takes place when sisters or brothers easily swap and wear each other's shoes and clothes, or they exchange clothing easily with their parents because they are nearly the same size. Done occasionally, this practice of swapping clothing is not troublesome, but as a repeated practice it can become quite an annoying and troubling disregard of personal boundaries.

In too many families, however, the confusion of personal boundaries goes much beyond the occasional swapping of articles of clothing. In one family the parents had no privacy for their bedroom. The doorknob on the parents' bedroom door needed repair. The door was removed several years ago for the repair, and was never replaced. Consequently, the children were permitted any time to observe or listen to whatever was happening in their parents' bedroom. In many such families where the boundaries are fuzzy, everyone's problems become everybody else's problems. There is little or no privacy, whether psychological or physical.

Persons reared in such families often have a hard time,

when they are adults, in distinguishing their own emotional boundaries from the emotional problems of other people. Thus they find themselves often overinvolved in other people's problems, or overconcerned and involved in their children's problems. Frequently, such persons feel that others have to change in order for them to be happy. As a result they spend a lot of time trying to change other people, instead of developing their own security and self-esteem within themselves.

It is not unusual for persons with unclear personal boundaries to become professional counselors because they enjoy being involved so much in other people's problems, or they simply become the informal family, neighborhood, or church "counselor." Their personal boundaries have no doors that close; anyone can come into their life at any time, even three o'clock in the morning, and stay as long as they want. Such poor boundaries were characteristic of the woman who continued to do her husband's laundry and ironing even though he was living at another woman's apartment. He would leave his laundry at the front door, and his wife would dutifully do it and have it ready the next morning. Having no firm sense of personal boundary in her life, the woman could not protect her own dignity and self-esteem despite her husband's irresponsible and unfaithful behavior. Having personal boundaries without doors that close is poor self-care, and it leaves many persons vulnerable to much emotional stress as they try to live with so many other people's problems besides trying to manage their own personal life as well.

Another common example of inadequte personal stewardship and self-care is the life-style that assumes our emotions and our physical body are inexhaustible natural resources. We all know that until recently the same notion prevailed in this country; we assumed that the natural resources of clean water, forests, fresh air, and rich mineral deposits would always be with us. It is hoped that most of us now know better.

Many of the persons who go to see a counselor about the stress in their life give the impression that they think they can "burn the candle at both ends" emotionally and physically, and then they wonder why they feel so exhausted. Most people would not treat their car the way many people treat their own bodies and their own emotions. Automobiles require regular maintenance, and they run best when the oil is changed and lubrication occurs on schedule. Most of us know, too, that our cars will not perform properly if we drive them at speeds or in road and weather conditions beyond their capability.

Failure to keep one's work within reasonable limits is a common example of failure to care for oneself. Roger Burns wonders why he has difficulty relating to his family. He works long hours and tries to get by on four hours' sleep each evening. Sitting in the counselor's office, Roger stared straight ahead, blankly. When the counselor inquired how he was feeling, Roger admitted he was feeling a little tired. More than that, Roger was on the brink of complete exhaustion. And that pattern had gone on for several years in his life!

Workaholism is the term for our country's obsession for work which usually abuses our personal natural resources of mind, body, and spirit. Workaholics are often very virtuous people with noble goals and relentless discipline for ignoring the pains and pressures they take upon themselves. One such man recently sat in my office. His body aches most of the time in various places, and he is having difficulty sleeping. He told me: "I learned in my family and during my military service that I can work until I am tired and then push well beyond those limits. I was awake most of the night planning the next work project I am going to take on for our company."

The workaholics are the saints of the twentieth century. Wayne Oates, himself a self-confessed workaholic, makes the important observation that in our culture workaholism is regarded as something of a religious virtue, even a form of patriotism, and certainly the way to be "healthy, wealthy, and wise." Workaholism is such a virtue in our eyes, says Oates, that compulsive workers are the ones we regard as "the most likely to succeed." (Wayne E. Oates, *Confessions of a Workaholic: The Facts About Work Addiction,* p. 12; Abingdon Press, 1971.)

Dr. Tobias Brocher of the Menninger Foundation has seen many workaholics who have burned themselves out on the way to the top. Brocher says that such persons have much ambition and ability, but their desire for work is insatiable, even at the cost of losing their families. When they fail to get the promotion they want so badly, they slip into a serious depression and discover too late that their spouse and children have left or are strangers. (Phillip S. Brimble interviewed Brocher for the article "Burned-out Young Lions Litter the Corporate Jungle," *Menninger Perspective,* Vol. 11, No. 1, Spring 1980, p. 12.)

Probably it is success, or some form of success, that tempts most of us to push our personal resources repeatedly beyond their limits. In college, it was the illness, mononucleosis, that supposedly identified the students who were pushing themselves too hard without getting adequate rest and care for their bodies. But the patterns continue further into adulthood. One man wisely observed that there are many symbols of success which, like Boy Scout merit badges, lure us to collect as many of those trophies of success as our personal resources will tolerate—and all for what?

For others, it is the sense of duty that prompts them to forget they have personal limitations and they cannot save the world. Churches and communities have virtually inexhaustible needs for the dutiful and well-meaning persons who give many, many hours of volunteer time. But such persons also invite burnout when their personal exhaustion and their disillusionment are rewarded with little evidence of accomplishment for all their efforts.

Responsible Christian wisdom recognizes that your personal resources of energy, enthusiasm, and physical strength are limited. You can wear yourself out, but there are not many causes that merit the intentional seeking of physical and spiritual burnout.

If you are to be a faithful Christian steward, you must take care of *all* the resources given to you, even your own mental, physical, emotional, and spiritual resources. You need to take care to protect your own wholeness, so that when you are called upon to give and to give deeply, you shall have the full gift to offer that is asked of you. You are your own greatest asset for a Christian life of loving service.

Essential Self-Care for Christians

Here is a brief checklist of four basic prerequisites if a Christian is to be ready for dealing with stress. The first requirement for Christian self-care is *cultivating a vital spiritual center.* I can say clearly that my own resources for coping with stress have been greatly diminished when I have lost for a while my faith perspective on my life and my responsibilities. Similarly, I have observed the same loss of balance in others when the spiritual dimension of their lives has been ignored or allowed to grow cold. Most significantly, when I lose the sense of the presence of the Christ, I am much less successful in my efforts to cope with my own anger and greed. Unchecked, it is my anger and my greed that increase my anxieties, multiply my worries, and disrupt my sleep too many hours of the night.

Also the vital sense of Christ at the center of your life helps you to keep essential priorities clear. Stress and burnout often occur because life is spent for things that matter very little. Christ at the center helps you to see much more readily where the true priorities and the legitimate urgencies really are. Most of the worries that keep us awake at night and the pressures that keep us going in so many different directions during the day will lose much of their demanding importance when Christ is at the spiritual center of your life.

Each person must take the responsibility to do whatever is necessary to cultivate a growing, enriching spiritual center. For many persons this requires regular church attendance as well as time for prayer, meditation, and study of Scripture. A woman recently commented that she was planning to memorize the entire Gospel of John, the fourth book in the New Testament. She explained that it would be a source of much reassurance to her to know the story of her Lord by heart. Most Christians will not choose to memorize a whole book of the Bible, but studying and recalling such passages as Psalm 23; Psalm 91; Psalm 121; Psalm 139:1–12; Matthew 5:1–12; Romans 8:28–39; and Philippians 4:4–7 can offer needed assurance, strength, and perspective for coping with the relentless demands on our strength and patience.

Your spiritual center will be rooted in the reality of God's love for you. Many Christians have great difficulty in recognizing that God really loves them. Instead of viewing themselves as being lovable, they basically view themselves as being so sinful as to be essentially unlovable. They believe that they are truly bad persons. In my own spiritual journey I have been greatly aided by seeing our Christian spirituality in a different and refreshing light. I have been helped to see more clearly the truth that above all else we are loved by God. God made us, and what he made he regarded as good. Despite how we fall short of his glory, he "so loved the world" that his love is still offered to us through Jesus Christ. Though we can never deserve it, we are loved. We are precious.

It is important that you as a Christian be able to make the self-affirmation "Through Jesus Christ, I am lovable, I am precious in God's sight!" That affirmation is the basis for all self-confidence, hope, and assurance for coping with the stress that threatens to overwhelm you.

Next on the checklist for Christian self-care is the necessity for *living by grace and not by guilt*. This guideline speaks to a very serious problem for many Christians. A friend of mine came to see me recently. She was characteristically out of breath, and she was talking with a steady stream of nonstop words tumbling out after each other. My friend's rapid speech pattern very well describes her life-style. She tumbles after herself from one hour to the next in order to get all the important, urgent, and necessary things done that are on her daily agenda. From an early age as a child she decided how to be a "good little girl," and she has been working very hard at it the rest of her life. She explained with a troubled sound to her voice: "If I don't get everything done, I will feel guilty. I feel guilty most of the time for what I haven't accomplished." Then, out of desperation because of the great amount of guilt and stress she is under all the time, she exclaimed, "I cannot go on like this any longer!"

You as a Christian, like my friend, may be following a legalistic spiritual pattern that is mainly an endless listing of "shoulds" and "oughts" if you are driven anxiously and exhaustingly through the day. This may be especially true if you feel guilty and uneasy when you have not completed everything you feel ought to be accomplished by the day's end. Another friend of mine, for whom the church has been central for most of her life, experienced several months of severe depression because of the countless "shoulds," "oughts," and "have tos" that were tyrannizing her life. While she was in psychotherapy, her wise counselor gave her the assignment of writing down all the things she "should" do each day. Being so dutiful, she came up with a very long list. There was hardly anything that she should not do! She wrote:

> I should floss my teeth.
> I should have a clean house.
> I should keep my husband and my children happy.
> I should go to church and Sunday school every Sunday.
> I should be on the worship committee at church.
> I should sing in the church choir.
> I should play the piano for Sunday school.

> I should not complain about how much time church activities take.
> I should have my parents and my husband's parents for Thanksgiving dinner.
> I should have my Christmas cards finished by December 10.
> Et cetera, et cetera, et cetera.

Reading that list, you are reminded of Jesus' criticism of the scribes and the Pharisees who urged others to work hard at their religion. Jesus said, "They bind heavy burdens, hard to bear, and lay them on men's shoulders; but they themselves will not move them with their finger" (Matt. 23:4). There is a scribe or a Pharisee living within many serious Christians, driving those Christians to live with such a great burden of inner rules and laws that they hardly ever know any peace.

Caring for yourself requires accepting the rich Christian message of grace, love, and acceptance. Then you will be in a position to learn that the harder you try to make yourself good or the more diligently you try to accomplish everything that "has to be done," the more you will realize that your goal cannot possibly be met. You are still left with the same conclusion that Paul reached, "For I do not do what I want, but I do the very thing I hate" (Rom. 7:15b). How wonderful, then, is the gospel message of grace that says we no longer need to be driven by guilt and the compulsion always to try just a little harder. *Responsible Christian self-care accepts the grace of God that sets us free from the tyranny of "should" and "ought."*

The third essential aspect of self-care for the Christian is *saying "yes" and "no" clearly without reluctance or guilt.* Our Lord spoke of the importance of saying a clear yes and no (Matt. 5:37a; see also James 5:12). You, however, may find it very difficult to say yes and no without feeling guilty. If so, you will be able to identify with much of what Manuel J. Smith says in his book *When I Say No, I Feel Guilty* (Dial Press, 1975).

One of the reasons you may be reluctant to say yes or no is because of the excessive and inappropriate responsibility which you take for others' feelings. Fearing you may hurt someone's feelings, you may not respect your own needs by setting clear limits. For the Christian, however, saying yes to others in love requires that you also be able to say yes to yourself as well!

I can readily say that for me it is not always easy to say yes and no. Not long ago it became apparent that too much stress was mounting up in my life, and that I had to make some decisions about my priorities. Saying yes to myself also meant saying yes to my family and saying yes to my job. Those priorities had to come first. I realized that I had to say no to other good things. I had to say no to a Bible class I was teaching, no to a church committee on adult education I was a member of, and no to an invitation to talk to a group of clergy about stress management. The decisions for me are rarely if ever between good and bad choices. They are usually between very important and attractive options. However, I knew that if I did not say a clear yes to my highest priorities and to my own mental and spiritual balance, I would not be offering my best to anyone.

Speaking a definitive yes or no is particularly important as you endeavor to keep clear commitments and communications with others. I remember being present when Pastor Fred Hanson was confronted during an adult Sunday school class by Harry Brown. Harry recommended that a committee from the board of deacons discuss with the pastor, before each Sunday school class, the material to be presented by the pastor in order to be certain the pastor was considering all points of view. Calmly, without hesitation, and with determination clearly evident in his tone of voice, Fred replied: "As long as I have the responsibility for leading the discussion in this class, I will make my own preparation ahead of time, and I will then welcome open discussion as a response from the class. But I will not meet with a special committee before the class."

The same definitive yes and no must be said when parents have to make the decision to place their teenage son or daughter in chemical dependency treatment against their child's will. A similar clear yes and no must be spoken when a spouse must make that agonizing decision to wait no longer for an estranged partner to return home and rebuild a marriage. Likewise, a firm yes and no must be declared when an employee has to confront an employer, risking dismissal but doing so because integrity and the difference between right and wrong are at stake.

Often saying a clear yes or no does not lower tension but rather may heighten feelings of animosity and misunderstanding. On the other hand, finally saying yes or no can clarify matters that have needed clarifying for a long time. Then the exhausting stress of indecision, which is often the worst kind of burden, can finally be set aside. *Responsible Christian self-care recognizes that there are limits to one's mental, spiritual, and physical strength. A clear yes or no that respects those limits is necessary for keeping stress manageable.*

Finally, responsible Christian self-care includes *being attentive to the physical needs of your body.* Donald B. Ardell calls such responsible self-care "high level wellness." (See both of Ardell's books: *High Level Wellness: An Alternative to Doctors, Drugs, and Disease;* Rodale Press, 1977; and *14 Days to a Wellness Lifestyle;* Whatever Publishing, 1982.) He rightly reminds us that "marvelous though it is, your body cannot, over the long haul of the years, resist and survive the punishment occasioned by disuse, misuse, neglect, and denial." (Ardell, *High Level Wellness,* p. 51.)

I am especially impressed by the fact that, in over ten years as a professional psychotherapist, I do not recall anyone ever coming to me for counseling who was at the time engaged in a *program of regular exercise!* My own conclusion is that persons who do have a program of regular exercise handle the stress in their lives fairly well for two reasons. They have to plan and manage their time sufficiently well in the first place in order to make a regular time for fifteen to forty-five minutes of exercise several times during the week. Secondly, the physical outlet, whether it is brisk walking, racquetball, jogging, or some other activity that elevates one's heartbeat, is an excellent way to clear the mind and work off the accumulated pressures of daily stress. Likewise, a return to regular exercise is often a very helpful first step to regaining management over excessive stress in one's life.

Every person whom I see for counseling first completes a medical history form. One of the questions asks the amount of caffeine consumed daily. It is amazing to me the number of people who come to counseling complaining that they cannot cope emotionally with the pressures at home and at work, and they see no connection between their nervousness and the eight to twenty cups of coffee or caffeinated soft drinks they are consuming each day! Similarly, persons who smoke, drink alcohol, or use other drugs need to consider what price they are paying for even the light or casual use of such chemicals. If you are going to be at your best for coping with the limitless pressures that confront you from one hour to the next, how can you justify the use of any chemicals that can radically reduce your capacity for managing stress?

You are the greatest asset God has given you for coping with stress! You have important physical, emotional, intellectual, and spiritual resources that will work well for you under pressure if you have taken good care of them. The question is the life-style you choose to live. The point has been well emphasized that an unhealthful life-style can be the cause of many physical symptoms of stress from hypertension to frequent flu and colds. (Duane R. Carlson, ed., *The Blue Cross and Blue Shield Guide to Staying Well,* p. 3; Contemporary Books, 1982.) A responsible life-style, a healthful life-style, will give you a head start on dealing with stress and the threat of burnout.

Responsible Christian self-care takes very seriously the physical needs of the body God has given each of us. With your body functioning at its best, you will be much better able to manage stress and to avoid the exhaustion of burnout.

I do not remember where I saw it, but of course the saying is true that "God don't make no junk!" You are precious, you are lovable, you are worthy of great care.

Look out for yourself. Take very good care of yourself. It is a Christian responsibility and opportunity.

Chapter 3

Making All the Ends Meet

> There is a harassed, knife-edge quality to daily life. Nerves are ragged, and—as the scuffles and shootings in subways or on gas queues suggest—tempers are barely under hair-trigger control. Millions of people are terminally fed up.
> *Alvin Toffler*
> The Third Wave, *p. 382*
> *William Morrow & Co., 1980*

> Do not be conformed to this world but be transformed by the renewal of your mind, that you may prove what is the will of God, what is good and acceptable and perfect.
> *Romans 12:2*

My friend David Parker sat slumped over, his posture reflecting his inner exhaustion. I had invited him to stop by my home because I was greatly concerned about him. He told me about the pains in his hip and back. He also acknowledged that his repeated grouchiness over the past four months was increasingly hard for his wife and children to handle. He explained the source of his stress, saying: "I can't get any business, and my employees are demanding that I pay them on time. I've taken on another part-time job, and I hardly get any sleep before I have to go back to my regular job. I don't let myself get tired anymore; I just keep on working long past I am tired. It's the only way I know to make ends meet."

David and I had been friends long enough that I could easily ask my next question. "How does your faith provide you resources for dealing with all the stress that you are trying to carry?" His face showed hardly any feeling, and his voice sounded far away as he replied: "God is not very real for me now. I used to go to church, but now all I know is that I have to keep working. I know that if I don't slow down my busy pace, I will finally get myself out of this hole." My friend's voice was flat; the joy of life had long ago flowed from his spirit and heart.

David's personal turmoil reminded me of the crises I have seen many families experience. Unfortunately, it is not an unusual occurrence for a teenager to get in trouble with the law or to become chemically dependent; the entire family feels the pressures from such problems. Serious illness in one family member will send shock waves bounding through the life of each person in the family. Likewise, the loss of a job by the principal breadwinner, or injuries suffered in an accident, suddenly creates an emotional and spiritual crisis for the whole family.

Stress and Strain

It is during such times of family crisis that it can be so difficult to make all the ends meet. Stress drains physical, emotional, and spiritual energy, to say nothing of financial resources. Nerves are set on edge. Getting along with family members becomes more difficult because everyone is feeling tense. One person observed that the stress at such a time is multiplied because of two shocks. The first shock, he explained, is the realization that someone close to you is really in trouble with the police and the court system, or has nearly been killed in an automobile accident. "It's supposed to happen to other people, but you wake up and it dawns on you that it has happened right in your own family, in your own house!"

The second shock, he went on to describe, is the demanding stress of adjusting to meet the crisis. If your child is in conflict with school authorities or with the law, there are countless meetings to go to, which can be very emotionally draining and upsetting. If your family schedule has been tight before such a crisis occurs, suddenly your old urgencies are replaced by new emergencies. One father, whose son was suddenly diagnosed as chemically dependent and put in an outpatient treatment program, described the shock and stress in these words: "Up till then I had thought that my schedule was already quite full with relentless priorities. But the treatment program required participation by everyone in the family, so I had to suspend many important commitments and give major portions of my time to the treatment process. My own resources of time, energy and money were being stretched to their limits; I faced many days not knowing how I would make all those ends meet."

Making all the ends meet is the principal assignment you and I have from one day to the next. We somehow have to make the financial ends meet, plus making the ends meet as we cope with having so little time, so little patience, and countless demands from so many people. Even without the major calamities of losing your job or suffering with a terminal illness, the more "normal" everyday crises of leaking clothes washers, sick children, and trying to figure out what to fix for supper all place great stress and strain upon you. The shoelace that breaks when you are already fifteen minutes late can have a devastating effect upon how the rest of your day goes. Daily stress that arises naturally out of all the activities of a "normal" day can become quite overwhelming. For many of us it seems the "ends" of money, time, energy, and patience just do not meet often enough from one day to the next.

The world we must deal with is certainly relentless in its demands that we accommodate, be flexible, adjust, and respond to emergencies on a moment's notice. Nonetheless, our Christian faith calls us always to examine ourselves, indeed to consider seriously how we contribute and add to our stress and burnout by our own attitudes and behaviors.

Greg Thompson's problems help to illustrate how many of us create much of our own burdening stress. Greg was serious and desperate when he explained to me: "I cannot handle the stress in my life any longer, and I am about to lose my career and my family because of the crazy way I am living. I cannot manage my own life anymore." As Greg and I talked, it became readily apparent to both of us that he had managed to create the myth in his life and among those who knew him that he was *indispensable*. He had come to believe that nothing in his work could be done without his direct involvement, and he had also given the impression to many in his community that nothing could really be accomplished unless he was serving on the boards of the principal agencies. Up till then Greg had fooled himself with the other major myth in his life, namely, the delusion that *he could manage his life himself.* My assignment to Greg was for him to go back to his community and to his work colleagues and to admit to five persons that his life was unmanageable. He was to tell them that the stress in his life had gotten totally out of hand and that he was through trying to run his life himself—since obviously his way of running his life was not working very well for him!

Greg Thompson's struggle to deal with the excessive stress in his life illustrates certain Christian truths that can guide you in coping with the pressures in your own life. As Greg learned, the "distress" of the pressures in your life can create a "teachable" opportunity for you to see your life and your priorities from a new perspective. In the New Testament, the word "repentance" conveys the message of turning around, making a U-turn because you see that you have been going in the wrong direction. Indeed, in Paul's case his conversion was not complete until "something like scales" fell from his eyes and he regained his sight (Acts 9:18). On another occasion, Jesus healed a man who later explained simply, "One thing I know, that though I was blind, now I see" (John 9:25b).

Greg saw, as he had never seen before, the spiritual implications and consequences of how he was living his life. Similar learnings have come to others who have chosen a lifestyle that has placed intolerable stress upon themselves and upon those around them. It may be while you are recovering from a heart attack in the hospital, or it may be when you are trying to put the pieces of your marriage back together, that you suddenly see the picture of your life more clearly than you have ever seen it before. The pain in Greg's life because of his mental and physical exhaustion brought him to a place of spiritual renewal, because he had his eyes opened to the facts about his life he had been trying to avoid for a long time.

The chief fact Greg had been avoiding was that he was failing at his efforts to manage his own life. The same theme is addressed early in the Bible. If the story of Adam and Eve says anything about us, it makes it clear that we do not do well when we think we are in charge and can have things our own way. Adam and Eve did not manage things well by trying to do it all their own way, so the account goes, and they lost their paradise. The New Testament consistently reaffirms that only Jesus Christ is Lord. Our eyes are opened to much spiritual wisdom when we reach the point, perhaps in the moment of a profound, stressful crisis, of seeing that we are not in charge of our own lives. Despite our noblest efforts at being the "captain of our own ship" and "doing it our own way," we are nearest the truth for our lives when we can identify with Greg's confession, "I cannot manage my own life anymore."

My invitation to you is to examine those areas of your life, most likely where the stress is the greatest, where you are trying to run things yourself and not permitting Christ to be Lord. Where is it that you are reluctant to release your efforts to manage yourself, others, and your future? For many of us who are parents, it is difficult to stop managing our children's lives. Because we love them, we want them to benefit from our mistakes and our wisdom in order to assure their future happiness and success. Our anxieties as parents are well grounded when you consider all the ways a child may be hurt, injured, or fall under the influence of the wrong persons. Yet in many respects there is little you can do to guarantee your child's happiness and security.

Indeed, I have discovered that the more I try to control my children, the more resistant they become to my advice and parental wisdom. Not long ago I took a hot pan with a pizza on it from the oven and set it on the table in front of my younger teenage son. I quietly reminded him to wait a moment until the pan had cooled off. He muttered, "Sure," and then immediately proceeded to stick his fingers between the pan and the pizza. I shall never forget the look of both pain and embarrassment on his face in that brief moment. And he will never forget that experience either, but not because of anything I told him. I wish I could protect my sons from hurting themselves, but at some point I must remember that their security and safety are finally in the Lord's keeping, and their lives are not mine to control from one minute to the next.

Just as parents must learn the spiritual truth that they cannot control their children's well-being, even so must children often learn, in their later years, that they cannot control their aging parents. Many middle-age children are discovering that there is much to worry about as their parents struggle with the infirmities and illnesses that accompany the aging process. Though children try to reassure their parents that they will come across the country whenever they are needed, aging parents ordinarily prefer to retain management of their own lives. If you are excessively worried with the problems of an aging parent, it may well be time for you to let the Lord manage more of that important personal concern.

Another area of major stress for many persons is the personal or domestic problems of their neighbors or friends. Recently in an adult Sunday school class I was leading a discussion on Christian marriage. One person asked, "What do you do when a couple you are close to is on the verge of a separation and divorce?" Others added that a similar question was on their mind regarding close relatives who were having serious marital problems. The truth is that as a Christian you will naturally be very concerned and do all that can reasonably be done to help. But in many such instances the best help is to recommend a competent marriage counselor to such persons and then leave their future in the Lord's hands. The temptation is to become overinvolved, to try to solve other people's problems, and to forget that it is not your place to manage their lives. Discovery of that spiritual truth can greatly ease the stress that comes with trying to save other people from their own problems.

The Christian faith also teaches you that Christ is Lord of the future. But what about the anxieties many of us have for our vocational, professional, and financial futures? Certainly it is advisable to engage in realistic planning for future needs, and to make wise financial decisions so that future family and personal responsibilities can be met with confidence. But it is another matter when your anxieties for the future lead you to spend years exhausting yourself in the climb to the top, wherever that is, meanwhile sacrificing personal health and family relationships.

I remember a man who came for counseling because he was experiencing some troubling personal confusion. Part of his problem was that at age thirty-five he had already made it to the top in his profession. Now he did not know what to do. Moreover, being at the top was not all that he had thought it would be. So he had come for counseling to begin discovering what his life was really supposed to be about besides trying to secure his future. There can be that profound moment of spiritual truth when you discover that you are not the lord of your own life and certainly not the lord of your own vocational and professional future. Despite who your broker is, you cannot manage what the future is going to bring you.

Another major source of stress for many persons occurs right in their family because at least one person is the "manager" of the household. Some families have virtually taken a vote and elected one person as the sergeant who tells others when to get up, clean up, wash up, and eat up. Usually the person chosen for such a family role seems to enjoy being in control. But the problem with such a role is that everyone else in the family pays little attention to the one who is supposedly in control. Consequently, the one in charge has all the stress of trying to organize the family, and the accompanying frustration usually results in much nagging of the other family members. In such a situation, everyone feels a great deal of stress and tension.

You and I invite much stress into our lives when we forget that there is one Lord and that we cannot really manage our own lives, much less the lives of other people. If you are presently under a great deal of stress, even fearing the possibility of burnout, then maybe you are near to claiming the truth for yourself that there is Another who can manage your life better than you can. Indeed, nothing less than an act of surrender can release one from the burden of feeling that one is indispensable and must be in charge. Only a spiritual surrender permits one to let go of the anxieties that have all the appearances of being urgencies and emergencies. But that surrender is possible because the good news is that Christ is Lord, and we no longer need to keep hold of the burden of trying to run everything ourselves.

Many persons today affirm their spiritual surrender by praying the Serenity Prayer:

> God grant me
> the serenity to accept the things I cannot change,
> courage to change the things I can, and
> wisdom to know the difference. Amen.

While I am saying that prayer, my thoughts have often flashed back to a Roman prison where a wise, patient man, his body bearing many scars, under threat of losing his life to an executioner, dictated these words confidently to his secretary:

> I have learned, in whatever state I am, to be content. I know how to be abased, and I know how to abound; in any and all circumstances I have learned the secret of facing plenty and hunger, abundance and want. I can do all things in him who strengthens me. (Phil. 4:11b–13)

Paul was kindly trying to reassure his friends that, despite the severity of his circumstances, he had more than enough resources for meeting the stress in his life.

He showed in many ways that he had been through an extraordinary school where he had learned the lesson for dealing with whatever life threw at him. That school was in the shadow of a cross and somewhere on a road to Damascus, and the lesson learned was surrender to the Christ and living Lord of life. In that surrender Paul had gained the perspective for viewing the priorities in his life correctly, for discovering that much he had worried about and been so discontent about before was not what really mattered anymore.

While I am wondering if I will ever make ends meet in my life, Paul saw all the ends meeting in his life with a victory that gave him a good deal more than what we call confidence or serenity!

Simplicity

Richard Foster has described his discovery of Christian simplicity. At the heart of his discovery was the realization that there is far more to the Christian life than the living of a frantic, scattered life-style. Foster was able to reclaim for himself that vibrant spiritual center, where Christ dwells within, that enabled him to say yes and no in such a way that he could once again live with less confusion and greater peace. Foster addresses the issue directly:

> We feel strained, hurried, breathless. The complexity of rushing to achieve and accumulate more and more frequently threatens to overwhelm us; it seems there is no escape from the rat race.

Christian simplicity frees us from this modern mania. It brings sanity to our compulsive extravagance, and peace to our frantic spirit. It liberates us from what William Penn called "cumber." It allows us to see material things for what they are—goods to enhance life, not to oppress life. People once again become more important than possessions. Simplicity enables us to live lives of integrity in the face of the terrible realities of our global village. (Richard J. Foster, *Freedom of Simplicity*, p. 3; Harper & Row, 1981)

The promise of such simplicity is incredible when we consider the time and the culture in which we live. A man recently told me about his digital wristwatch, a product of our technological computer age. The watch was rather inexpensive and made a perfect birthday gift from his wife just a few years ago. As a result of the latest advances in the production of silicon chips and quartz crystals, his watch keeps him on time to within two or three seconds of accuracy. Moreover, if he pushes the right button a tiny light goes on so he can read the digital figures and see within two or three seconds what time it really is in the middle of the night!

But to operate this watch and to take full advantage of all its features, the man explained that he has to consult the owner's manual to remember how to use all the various modes. He particularly finds it embarrassing to try to reset the watch, the procedure is so precise and complicated. If he forgets which button to push at the right moment, he will lose several hours in the blink of an eye. He says he occasionally becomes nostalgic about the watch he received when he graduated from high school. It did not do anything spectacular; it just rested faithfully on his wrist for twenty years, the hands always circling within four or five minutes of the correct time. There were no buttons to push, but of course he could not read the watch in the dark, and it did not give him split times for road races, either!

Our way of life is so advanced we have developed the suspicion that if anything reflects simplicity it must be obsolete or an antique. Supposedly computers are going to simplfy our lives, but we are easily fooled if we believe that. Recently there was notice of some new software for home computers that will organize your refrigerator and your pantry and give you menus and recipes based on what you have in stock. It all sounds incredibly simple until you realize that the computer can do nothing until you spend the time entering into the computer all the items currently in your refrigerator and your pantry. Perhaps in that time you will have figured out for yourself what to do with four hard-boiled eggs, a few green onions, some mayonnaise, three boiled potatoes, and a little salt.

Nor is it just computers and gadgets that threaten to make life more complicated for us. There is also the more important matter of life-style. Where I live, it is commonplace for many families to have either a boat or a summer cabin or both. There are important benefits to being able to enjoy the out-of-doors in the summer, and families can have many happy times together spending a few weeks or weekends in the natural surroundings of woods and water. But I keep wondering where there is time to maintain and repair both a house and a cabin, to mow two lawns and drive fifty to two hundred miles between the two lawns for the privilege of mowing them. Yet our society places a high premium upon maintaining a standard of living that offers the opportunity to enjoy such privileges. The price we pay in added stress for such a life-style is altogether obvious. It was that price which prompted one couple to say about the years they owned their own boat, "The happiest two days we owned that boat were the day we bought it and the day we sold it!"

The purpose of the gospel is not to make our middle-class life-style a little easier for us. The purpose of the gospel is to announce the good news that Jesus Christ is the Lord of life. Where he does reign as Lord, most of life's priorities become wonderfully ordered in such a way that there is an unprecedented peace and simplicity at the center. If you are going to recover a Christian simplicity, it will require a new agenda and a new set of values different in most ways from the people around you. That was just the point Paul was making: "Do not be conformed to this world but be transformed by the renewal of your mind, that you may prove what is the will of God, what is good and acceptable and perfect" (Rom. 12:2). Christian renewal that lives beyond burnout is based on a total change of heart and mind. That is where you shall find Christian simplicity and peace and serenity!

Someone will certainly ask: "How do I get this simplicity? How do I do it?" The answer, of course, is whether or not you are prepared to have Christ and his Spirit at the center of your life. And that is a very personal matter between you and your Lord. With Christ at the center of your life, you will begin to see many of your motives in a new light. Consequently, these may become very important and illuminating questions for you:

1. Does my behavior clearly show to the most important people in my life that I love them and care for them?
2. Is my need for success and achievement necessary to bolster a sagging sense of self-esteem?
3. Do I fail to have clear priorities for my life because I am afraid of offending people?
4. Do I keep myself unnecessarily busy so I can feel that I am needed by other persons?
5. Do I speak a clear yes and no based on my Christian values and commitments?

Of course it is not possible ever to judge the degree of Christian commitment and simplicity in another person's life. However, there is much evidence from other people's lives that they are living out of a Christian center that does not allow them to be conformed to this age and culture. For example, there are those who make certain sacrifices in order to remain a one-car family, a decision that often means one adult or both adults will ride a bicycle to work. In some families the decision has been made that clothing will be bought at a consignment or secondhand shop, even though the family easily has the means to purchase all its clothing new from major department stores. While many justify the expense of central air conditioning, some families maintain that their values do not require such an expenditure even though their budget could readily afford it. And one cannot forget the sight of those who, unlike most of the rest of us living in Minnesota, have clearly made the decision not to purchase a snowblower. Instead, they shovel through twelve to eighteen inches of snow, getting the benefit of exercise the rest of us would rather avoid.

Christian simplicity is also taking the time to picnic with friends or one's family next to a lake, or perhaps to take a vacation where there is no radio, television, or newspaper. Christian simplicity is the decision to emphasize and nurture those values in your life that sustain human relationships and to care wisely for the resources of your mind, body, spirit, and the environment in which you live. Christian simplicity is the peace that comes from living in harmony with God, with your neighbors and your natural environment, and, just as important, with yourself.

So the Ends Will Meet

Counselors and psychologists know that there is one invariable characteristic about human nature: we all want the benefits without having to make the personal changes necessary to get them. This point was well illustrated by Bill Norton when he went to see a counselor because he was at the point of complete physical and mental exhaustion. Bill recognized something was drastically wrong in his life because he could not sleep at night, he had lost his interest in food, and on a recent business trip that put a great deal of pressure on him he had been so preoccupied with his problems he missed a plane flight and thus a crucial meeting for his company. During that first session, Bill told the counselor he knew that he was near collapsing because of the irresponsible way he was managing his life. He declared, "I know this has to come to an end!"

Bill scheduled another counseling session a week later. When the time for that next session arrived, Bill was a few minutes late, and then he began by saying he could not stay more than five minutes because of another commitment on his calendar. But he said he wanted to schedule another counseling session. However, only a half hour before that next session Bill's secretary called the counselor to say Bill could not keep the appointment because he needed to see one of his business customers. The secretary said that Bill wanted to schedule another session for the next week. The day for that counseling session arrived, but Bill did not appear at the counselor's office. When the counselor called Bill the next day, Bill was very apologetic, saying he had forgotten the appointment because so many business pressures were on his mind. The counselor never heard from Bill again.

Bill Norton's case illustrates how much most of us resist seriously changing the habits of our personal life-style, even though we know that our personality and behavioral patterns create very distressing problems for ourselves. The apostle Paul clearly saw this characteristic within himself and recognized it as a serious obstacle to living a faithful life: "For I do not do the good I want, but the evil I do not want is what I do" (Rom. 7:19). If we are honest, most of us Christians will acknowledge our reluctance to take the steps and make the essential changes in our behavioral patterns that will enable us to manage our stress and burnout more effectively.

If you are to change, what may motivate you to take the steps for change that you have avoided until now?

1. A medical crisis may force you to recognize that unless

you handle your stress much differently your health may be seriously endangered. Persons who never thought they could quit smoking have stopped promptly with no questions asked after a heart attack or after they have been diagnosed as having emphysema. Likewise, Paul Larson, a man who has always weighed over two hundred pounds, has lost nearly twenty pounds and watches his diet very closely now because his doctor has told him that he is a "borderline diabetic."

2. You may be sufficiently motivated to change because all your hard work, which has created so much stress and burnout in your life, really has not brought you any satisfying rewards. You have asked the question "What's it all about?" and there is no longer any satisfying answer. This loss of purpose can come to the business person who has been very successful and who now finds little joy in what has been accumulated over the years. The same loss of interest in work and life can come, also, to persons who have given much of their life to helping others, namely, such professionals as nurses, teachers, and counselors. Housewives who have spent twenty or twenty-five years rearing a family may also be shocked to find themselves asking the same question: "What's it all about? The kids only come home when they need me for something." Disillusionment can be an important motivator for prompting growth changes in your spiritual and mental outlook.

3. You may decide it is time to make major changes in your management of stress because the people around you are paying too high a price. You may be comfortable with erratic work hours, irregular meal schedules, and sixty- to seventy-five-hour workweeks, but family members, work colleagues, or employees under you may be frantic because of your irresponsible pace and failure to keep to a reasonable schedule. You may think it is simply "their problem" that they cannot adjust to your idiosyncrasies, but you may decide it is your problem when family members, friends, and work

colleagues say they are relieved when you are not around so their own life can settle down to normal.

4. Excessive alcohol or chemical use is a sign that your personal stress management is not working well for you. Hugh Jensen was never a heavy drinker and only had one or two social drinks whenever he was with friends. But Hugh noticed when he took his new job that every Friday evening, and a couple nights during the week, he would come home and pour himself two stiff drinks in order to relax. This pattern continued for about eight months, when Hugh suddenly realized that alcohol was the only means he had for relaxing from the tension of his new job. Though he was not in fear of becoming an alcoholic, Hugh decided that he would sharply reduce his consumption of alcohol. Instead of drinking, he began walking three miles every night after work to clear his mind and release the tension from his body.

5. Another important motivator for change is the realization that your spiritual resources are drained and that whatever faith you once had is no longer meaningful for you. This condition of spiritual "malaise" is reminiscent of the concerned man who approached Jesus asking what he must do to have eternal life. When Jesus suggested that he keep the commandments, the man said he had already been faithful about observing the commandments. He knew that there was more to having a vital faith than what he was experiencing presently in his own life. (Mark 10:17–22.) The sense that your own faith has grown cold and lifeless may be a strong motivator for you now to make significant growth changes in your life.

The reasons that persons seek spiritual renewal for coping with stress and burnout are always varied. But the question that needs to be answered by each of us remains the same. It is the question that Jesus put to the invalid who had been ill for thirty-eight years and who was waiting to be healed by the waters in the pool called Beth-zatha. Jesus asked the man, "Do you want to be healed?" (John 5:6b.) It is a very important question because, surprisingly, quite often we do not want to be healed of our excessive stress and the spiritual burnout we have learned to tolerate. Renewal for living beyond burnout will not come to those who do not want to make the changes such renewal requires.

One approach to making all the ends meet in your life draws upon the two principal Christian resources, prayer and the supportive fellowship of the church, the body of Christ. Prayer is an especially helpful resource when through our prayers we learn to focus on one day at a time, recovering that grace of simplicity Jesus pointed to when he reminded his followers, "Let the day's own trouble be sufficient for the day" (Matt. 6:34b). Moreover, prayer, whether it be in the quiet of your own room or in the context of public worship, continually lifts up before you the fact that the world is not yours to run, but rather the world is a place in which you are called upon to be patient and obedient. When in prayer you ask Jesus to show you what should have the highest priority in your life, most often you will discover that much of what you hurry to get accomplished is usually not what is of the highest value when measured against the priorities of the Kingdom of God. This, you recall, was the learning for Martha when she was being so busy about being a good hostess and complained to Jesus that her sister, Mary, was sitting idly. Jesus' reply to Martha confronts you whenever you feel there is so much that you "must" get done: "Martha, Martha, you are anxious and troubled about many things; one thing is needful. Mary has chosen the good portion, which shall not be taken away from her" (Luke 10:41–42).

Though the simple act of slowing down to sit, kneel, or stand in one place long enough to say a prayer can ease your stress, the purpose of prayer is not for its accompanying relaxation benefits. The purpose of prayer is to connect your spirit with the larger Spirit of our loving God. The invitation for you to "be still, and know that I am God" (Ps. 46:10a) clearly states that the purpose of prayer is to help you recover the proper perspective about who God is and whose world it really is. Relaxation exercises of themselves can be important resources for managing stress; prayer helps you to be quiet so you can discover once again what really is important for the spiritual priorities in your life.

Tom Wilson found a unique approach to prayer that was a helpful way for him to become still within himself. Sitting in a comfortable chair, Tom inhaled a deep breath and tilted his head back as far as it would go. Then he exhaled, bringing his head forward until his chin nearly touched his chest. He did this several times, praying: "Lord, I exhale the tension and frantic anxiety that have me in turmoil. Lord, I inhale your peace, your strength, and your wisdom for directing my life so I can live sanely for you." After this breathing exercise, Tom also focused on his hands to help him keep in contact with Christ at the center of his life. With the palms of his hands down, he prayed, "Lord Jesus, I let go of my fear of losing my job, I release my anger with my supervisor, I let go of my anxiety that we shall not have money for Mike's college education next year." Then, turning his palms upward, he assumed the attitude of receiving from God. He prayed silently, "Lord Jesus, I am open to your acceptance of me, I am open to your support, I permit you now to run my life instead of me trying to do it." (For a fuller discussion of these and other meditation exercises, see Richard J. Foster, *Celebration of Discipline: The Paths to Spiritual Growth,* pp. 24–29; Harper & Row, 1978.)

Before Tom could use the supportive resources of the body of Christ, it was necessary for him to clarify through prayer his needs and objectives for reducing the stress in his life. The procedure that was followed by Tom is useful for many persons if they fully intend to manage their stress more effectively and avoid burnout. You too may find it beneficial. First, Tom made an *I need to . . .* list of the areas in his life where growth and change were needed. Tom's sense of Christian value and commitment, clarified and reinforced through prayer, helped him to focus sharply on the areas of greatest need. He kept his list to only seven principal concerns so his efforts toward change and growth would not become too scattered. Tom's list looked like this when he had finished:

I NEED TO ...
1. Take better care of myself by having greater simplicity in my life so I am not so tired and hard to live with so much of the time.
2. Lose the excessive weight I am carrying around.
3. Have more quality time with Donna when I am not so preoccupied with my work problems.
4. Get some kind of exercise on a regular basis.
5. Recover a greater sense of spiritual balance and direction for my life.
6. Do something about the fearfulness and guilt I feel when I try to say no when my boss or others put unreasonable demands on me.
7. Have more friends whom I can talk with and have fun with or share some of my concerns with when things are not going well for me. Right now Donna is my only friend, and that puts too much of a burden on her and does not feel right to me.

The next essential step for Tom was to translate his *I need to . . .* list into specific and concrete commitments that had time deadlines. Making this list of commitments was harder for Tom to do than he had first thought it would be. He found that it was particularly difficult to avoid vague generalities, but he finally constructed the following specific and realistic list. He was also encouraged because he could see that by following through with these commitments the overall level of stress in his life would be greatly reduced. Tom began his list with the two important words *I will,* not "I will try."

I WILL . . .
1. Reduce all my church commitments, starting next month, so that I do not attend more than five evening church functions or committee meetings per month.
2. Follow the diet plan which my medical doctor gave me two months ago, starting next Monday.
3. Take Donna out on a "date" at least once a month, starting next month, without the kids coming along.
4. Walk at a quick pace for thirty minutes, three times a week, starting in two weeks.
5. Attend the "Basic Steps in Christian Devotion" class being taught by Pastor Smith, starting in three weeks.
6. Take an assertiveness training course, offered through the local school district adult education department, within six months.
7. Take Bob Jackson and Chuck Taylor to lunch individually and let them know I value their friendship and want to share common concerns with them. I will do that with both of them within four weeks.

One more step remained for Tom if he was serious about living beyond the stress and burnout in his life. A major resource for every Christian is to draw upon the loving support of others in the church. In I Corinthians 12 and 13, Paul expands on the image of the body of Christ and the rich dimensions of the nature of love. Those two chapters reflect essential resources available within the fellowship of the church. Christians have known it to be true since Jesus' ministry, and counselors and psychologists have also more lately discovered the same principle, that desired changes in people's lives are more likely to occur when they receive love and support from others for those positive changes.

The fact is that many Christians are greatly troubled about the amount of stress in their lives, but few see much if any change really occur for the better. *Those who do experience positive change and growth in their lives have usually had the encouraging support of others.* Because Tom recognized his need for accountability and support, he wisely chose three persons, including his pastor and two other friends at church, whom, in the spirit of Christian trust and concern, he decided to tell about his list of seven commitments and his intention to make important changes in his life-style and relationships with others.

When Tom shared his list of commitments with those three persons, he asked them if they would be willing to have him report back to them every three or four months regarding his progress on his list of commitments. Because his objectives were so specific, it would be easy for him to say whether or not he had accomplished the changes he wanted to make. By choosing to *go public* and declare his intentions to others, Tom made it very unlikely that he would fail to keep the important commitments he had made to himself. By permitting others to give him support and encouragement, Tom was following the spiritual principle "Bear one another's burdens, and so fulfil the law of Christ" (Gal. 6:2). Tom recognized that if he was to recover a life with greater simplicity and less destructive stress, he would have to be connected to others and to permit the "body of Christ" made up of other believers to be a significant support base for his intention to change his overstressed life-style.

Conclusion

Making ends meet as you cope with innumerable pressures requires a spiritual surrender that accepts reality and confronts the delusion that you can manage your own life yourself. Your Christian faith calls, on a daily basis, for continuing surrender of your own attempt to control everything that creates so much anxiety and worry for you. Certainly Jesus was very serious about his teaching and invitation: "Therefore I tell you, do not be anxious about your life, what you shall eat or what you shall drink, nor about your body, what you shall put on. Is not life more than food, and the body more than clothing?" (Matt. 6:25). And behind his invitation is the necessity for increasing the depth of your surrender and your willingness to let God be in charge.

The essential promise of the gospel is that through spiritual surrender we are renewed to live beyond burnout. It is an amazing promise, but after we surrender, the ends do begin to meet and all the pieces fall into place, mainly because we no longer are trying so hard to do it all our own way.

Chapter 4

Beyond Easy Answers

> In Christ, that is, in humanity's true possibility, which is by no means self-evident, suffering summons our self-confidence, our boldness, our strength. Our oneness with love is indissoluble. To learn to suffer without becoming the devil's martyrs means to live conscious of our oneness with the whole of life. Those who suffer in this way are indestructible. Nothing can separate them from the love of God.
>
> *Dorothee Soelle*
> Suffering, *p. 141*
> *Fortress Press, 1975*

> We were so utterly, unbearably crushed that we despaired of life itself.
>
> *II Corinthians 1:8b*

Despair inevitably accompanies and hastens burnout. Despair rules the human spirit that has lost all hope. Despair is the stage of burnout that concludes, "Life is pointless."

I shall never forget my first experience as a pastor, quite a few years ago, of looking directly into the eyes of despair and spiritual burnout. Alice Morris was an ill-looking, frail woman who lived in a dimly lighted efficiency apartment that had hardly any furniture except a bed over against the wall. Alice was in an extreme state of desperation; she was ready to die. She was angry at me because I represented the church, and she felt that the church had abandoned her. At least none of the ministers she had tried to call all day would come to see her; never mind that she did not belong to any church. Alice was suffering through the advanced stages of Parkinson's disease. Her own daughter had recently come into the apartment and taken most of Alice's clothes out of the dresser and the closet. She was too ill to fix her own food. Alice looked right at me and told me that she had nothing to live for and that she would just as soon die. I do not know why I said it, but I replied that dying was certainly one of her choices.

Everything in Alice's life had fallen apart. She was in the grip of despair; no longer were there any easy answers for her. She had no more resources for coping with the mounting stress. Life had burned right out from underneath her.

One way to understand the effects of burnout is to think of the various stages of mental, physical, and spiritual exhaustion. LeRoy Spaniol suggests that burnout be considered in three stages. ("Teacher Burnout," *Instructor,* Vol. 88, No. 6, Jan. 1979, p. 57.) He says that first-degree burnout is mild and is characterized by short-lived bouts of irritability, fatigue, worry, and frustration. Second-degree burnout is moderately severe and is similar to first-degree, but it lasts for two weeks or more. Third-degree burnout is severe and is accompanied by physical ailments such as ulcers, chronic back pain, and migraine headaches.

It is commonplace for despair to be experienced at any one of those three levels of burnout. Hopelessness can overtake a person for just a few hours or a few days. The hopelessness may stem from a crisis in one's marriage or family, or from a critical problem arising in one's work. However, when no solution to the problem becomes evident, despair continues for weeks and months. Indeed, a person may be struggling with a profound sense of despair and not be fully aware of the depth of the hopelessness. Such a person may simply be aware that something very serious seems to be wrong but be unable to name what the problem is.

Despair often results in prayers for easy answers. Wayne Oates has written about the spiritual problem being faced by

Beyond Easy Answers

the despairing person who asks, "How long, O Lord, how long?" Oates reminds us that despair prompts us to offer prayers reflecting our helplessness while we plead for a miracle to rescue us from our plight. (Wayne E. Oates, *Pastor's Handbook,* Vol. I, p. 59, Christian Care Books; Westminster Press, 1980.)

Struggling with the burnout of despair can be especially difficult for Christians, because of the temptation to look for easy answers. I remember well when Gary Sommers came to see me about a very difficult situation he was struggling with at work that had been getting him down for more than a year. Gary had been reared in the church, and his faith was a very serious matter for him, often bringing him consolation and support. When he came to see me he said, "I have read all through the Bible for the promises that say whatever we ask for will be given to us." Then Gary quoted these passages:

> Ask, and it will be given you; seek, and you will find; knock, and it will be opened to you. For every one who asks receives, and he who seeks finds, and to him who knocks it will be opened. Or what man of you, if his son asks him for bread, will give him a stone? Or if he asks for a fish, will give him a serpent? If you then, who are evil, know how to give good gifts to your children, how much more will your Father who is in heaven give good things to those who ask him! (Matt. 7:7–11)

> Truly, I say to you, whoever says to this mountain, "Be taken up and cast into the sea," and does not doubt in his heart, but believes that what he says will come to pass, it will be done for him. Therefore I tell you, whatever you ask in prayer, believe that you have received it, and it will be yours. (Mark 11:23–24; see also John 15:7; I John 3:22; 5:14–15)

No one could have prayed any more earnestly than Gary, as he asked for some kind of divine intervention that would resolve the dreadful problem in his life. Similar prayers have been offered by parents caring for children with severe, chronic illnesses or handicaps. Married partners often live at the point of despair for countless years, asking God somehow to make a difference so they can live without pain, anguish, and abuse.

Gary wanted to know. What was he to do with God's silence? It is often in what seems to be God's silence that the human soul feels overwhelmed with despair, for where is there hope for prayers that hear no response from God?

Something More than Answers

There is persuasive evidence in the Bible that indicates God is reluctant to deal with our despair by offering simple answers or quick solutions. Job's experience, recorded for us in the Old Testament, is certainly a notable case in point. Job was a blameless and upright man who suddenly found he had lost nearly everything that was precious and valuable to him. He lost his wealth, and his sons and daughters perished in a great windstorm. And if that tragedy was not enough, he was also afflicted with oozing sores that covered every part of his body. His despair was without measure; only death made sense to him.

> Why is light given to him that is in misery,
>   and life to the bitter in soul,
> who long for death, but it comes not,
>   and dig for it more than for hid treasures;
> who rejoice exceedingly,
>   and are glad, when they find the grave?
>   (Job 3:20–22)

Job's three "friends" came to urge Job to recognize that God was giving him what he deserved. Their religious answer for Job was to repent and to recognize how great his wickedness must be in view of the greatness of his personal suffering and tragedy. Instead, Job declared that he was a blameless man. Though despairing, Job refused to sell short his integrity. Indeed, as one assured of his own self-confidence, Job impatiently declared that he wanted to confront his God in order to declare his own righteousness.

It is righteous impatience, born out of profound loss and suffering, that made Job reject all the advice and pious platitudes offered by his friends. Job did not want answers, nor was he prepared to say he deserved to suffer so unbearably. His integrity made him ask for something more; in his despair he wanted God himself, not just what we call answers and advice.

There is one word for what Job was doing with his despair: *wrestling.* Paul Scherer has called it "staying with it when you are down, and everybody else has made off," your "lonely, gallant wager that God is true." (Paul Scherer, Exposition of Job, *The Interpreter's Bible,* Vol. 3, p. 1159; Abingdon Press, 1954.) Job was wrestling with God and life and all that was good inside him, and he could not let go of that. Wrestling like that is at the heart of the Christian's despair. The encounter in such wrestling is with God, and in such an encounter there is more called forth from you than the pious humility we usually call patience. Rather, what is called forth from you is the courage to keep on holding on because God is refusing to let go of you!

That is why despair is a spiritual turning point. Indeed, in the midst of your despair, precisely because your despair is a wrestling with God, you may well be closer to God than at any other time of your life. One readily calls to mind Jacob's experience when he was despairing over the approaching confrontation with his brother Esau. That night Jacob wrestled with a divine being whom Jacob identified as God. That deep, exhausting wrestling was such a turning point for Jacob that his name was changed because he was changed. Thereafter he was known as Israel, which means "God rules." (Gen. 32:22–32.)

Despair can be a powerful and creative spiritual turning point in your life, *even though you sense that you are far from God and do not feel particularly religious or pious at the time of your despair!* Some persons can readily identify with the psalmist and talk with God in their despair, even about the distance between them and God.

> My God, my God, why hast thou forsaken me?
> Why art thou so far from helping me, from the words of my groaning?
>
> (Ps.22:1)

However, you may not even feel like praying when you are deeply despairing. In your hopelessness, the former religious practices may not hold meaning, and it may seem that there is no way to find God, much less find a way out of your dilemma. It is not unusual for persons who have been active in the church for many years to find themselves for months, or even years, to be withdrawn from the church during a time of crisis and spiritual exhaustion. I have known such persons who later have returned to assume quite an active role in the life of a congregation, and even go to seminary and become ordained clergy!

When you are far from God, God is not necessarily far from you. Even if you choose to hide from God in the deep darkness of your own despair, "even the darkness is not dark to thee" (Ps. 139:12a). There is no place, there is no human condition, where one can flee from God. "Whither shall I go from thy Spirit?" (Ps. 139:7a) the psalmist asks. The answer is nowhere. In your despair you are always wrestling with God to discover God's unfolding purposes for your life. And in those purposes there is ordinarily so much more than simply the answers you were seeking!

God Enters Our Despair

The final evidence that God does not offer simple answers for despair is set on a cross so we cannot miss it against that darkening, terrible sky. The cross was never meant to be God's easy answer. The cross is where God wrestled, struggled with his own blood against everything that has ever created despair in the human heart. The cross means that, instead of an answer, God puts his own life on the line. God enters our despair. God in Christ dies under the weight of our despair. We are not alone in our despair; there is Another who wrestles, who struggles, who endures beside us and for us.

When we are despairing, God is always giving us more, much more than the quick, simple solution that we are so sure will relieve us and make it all right. Instead, he himself is standing there like the Stranger in Fyodor Dostoevsky's *The Brothers Karamazov*. The Stranger came to those suffering from inhuman tortures under the fifteenth-century Inquisition in Seville, Spain. He stood quietly, powerful and unmoved, confronting with a steady, knowing gaze those bringing such pointless terror and suffering upon other human beings. It is that Stranger, with the nail prints in his hands and feet, who defines with his own life the patient endurance that outlasts despair.

Would you believe that I first learned about such endurance from Alice Morris, whom I met that despair-filled evening in her efficiency apartment? About five years after first meeting Alice, she invited me to attend the convention of a service organization to which she belonged. Alice would not explain to me why she wanted me to attend a particular session of the convention, but it was evident she was quite excited about the purpose of that meeting.

When I arrived, it was soon apparent that someone was going to be given a special award. To my surprise, Alice was asked to come forward in her wheelchair. I discovered that Alice was being given special recognition for her outstanding work in collecting funds for children's hospitals. The presenter of the award went on to say that Alice had spent countless weeks and months, in her wheelchair, sitting on street corners collecting money for the service organization's project of funding children's hospitals. Then he told a story about Alice I can never forget. He recounted how Alice had determined one day that she had to cross the freeway, in order to get from one shopping center to another to collect more money from shoppers. Never mind that cars were rushing by at sixty miles an hour. Instead of going to a pedestrian overpass, Alice wheeled her chair onto the freeway with the full intention of stopping traffic so she could cross to the other side. The resulting traffic tieup on the freeway brought the sheriff, who continued to stop the traffic so Alice could complete her crossing in her wheelchair. The lady who not long before could not get out of her bed to fix her own meals was now determined not to let anything stand in her way from helping the children she loved so much! That day of her recognition, Alice taught me an unforgettable lesson about endurance, and about wrestling and struggling with despair.

The message of the gospel comes as particularly good news to the people who have good reason for despair and hopelessness. Missionaries often report that usually it is the lower classes, who are living marginally with so few resources for shelter, food, and clothing, who find hope and encouragement in the gospel for surviving beyond their desperate circumstances. It is no surprise that Jesus announced his ministry in his hometown by reading the passage from Isaiah 61:1–2. Jesus' mission was to the poor, the captives, the blind, and the oppressed. His purpose was to deliver those who have the greatest reasons for despairing!

Moreover, if you are to find Jesus, you do well to find him, yourself, among those who are despairing. Just one look at the figure upon that cross will show you in his eyes that he is one of those who despairs for mercy, love, and release from oppression. And when you reach out to touch another hurting human being, the eyes that meet yours should leave no doubt that you are encountering the one crucified for all who despair.

Alice had moved beyond her despair by her investment of herself in the needs of others. Whether or not she would have used the words, the Christ who freed her from her despair was waiting for her in the needs of the children she loved.

The New Testament is always speaking of holding on in spite of all the odds that have piled up against us. Paul reminds us that "suffering produces endurance" (Rom. 5:3), and also James tells us that through various trials the testing of your faith will result in steadfastness (James 1:3). Then there is the final word from John, calling us to hold on because he is able to see "a new heaven and a new earth" (Rev. 21:1). You are able to hold on, to endure through your despair, because God is holding on. Recently, Sandra Miller was describing an illness that had kept her in bed for two and half months. She said that she knew she was on at least a dozen prayer lists, and that people all around the country were counting on her to get well. When she did not want to go to the doctor, her husband got firm with her and made her go. Afterward, Sandra was grateful because so many people were pulling for her, including of course her husband and family. She exclaimed, "When so many are behind you, you decide you can't let them down."

That is why there is so much endurance woven through the New Testament. The gospel is saying that God himself is enduring with us, beside us, for us. The cross itself defines God's endurance for us, and that cross is planted in the middle of every human life. God is enduring not just the pain and despair that get us down, but God also is enduring the faithlessness on our part. We are the odds God is having to face and endure! But because God does endure with us and for us, like Sandra we cannot let ourselves, others, or God down.

The New Testament scholar William Barclay has vividly explained the meaning of the Greek word *hupomonē,* normally translated in the New Testament as "patience" or "endurance." He says that such faithful endurance does not wait passively, with its head bowed, until the storm is over. Instead, the gospel is always speaking of bearing hardship with a "blazing hope" that awaits the dawn. (William Barclay, *New Testament Words*, pp. 143–145; Westminster Press, 1974.)

Sam Gilbert fit just that Christian sense of enduring in spite of despair. As a result of cerebral palsy, Sam's face was distorted, his body was twisted, and his muscular movements were often uncontrolled, so he could not hold a steady eye contact with you as he talked. One was immediately moved to shock, sympathy, pity by being in Sam's presence. But inside Sam's profoundly handicapped body was a loving person with a very bright mind. He told a group of us on one occasion about his recurring bouts with despair, his periods of depression when suicide looked so inviting. Nonetheless, he was living one day at a time, in spite of the cruel stares he had to tolerate wherever he went. Sam's despair had taught him how to hold on with courage and dignity.

Bob Cooper and Ruth Hall each have struggled with the despair that comes often with being a single parent. Bob's wife died some years ago, and he is parenting three children. Ruth lost her husband many years ago in a tragic accident, and she has had to rear five children by herself. The problems and the discouragement faced by single parents like Bob and Ruth are quite common. There are questions like: Where do you find help for decision-making, so you are not always having to make crucial decisions on your own? How do you stand up to the continuing need for steady, firm discipline? And how can a single parent ever find time to be alone with private thoughts and feelings, without being constantly on call? It is the fighting among the children that brings on despair for both Bob and Ruth as much as anything else. Yet they have shown what endurance is, endurance with struggling and wrestling when there are no quick, magical answers to the despair-filled prayers.

Despair is the Christian's occasion to wrestle, in the final analysis, with God. It is out of such wrestling that endurance is born. When there are no answers, it is the wrestling with God that is the only way the Christian can live and not die. Living beyond despair would not be possible for any of us, had not God given us more than answers—the gift of himself always with us in the midst of the struggle.

Opportunity Beyond the Despair

By all human standards there should be no gospel, no Christian faith. With Jesus' death there was every reason for his followers and disciples to return in despair to their former labors and to forget their last three years with their Lord. In fact, there is no human explanation for how or why the Christian faith could continue and thrive after Jesus' death.

The problem with human despair is that it is just as shortsighted as it is certain that all hope is lost. Despair is always quick to draw discouraging conclusions before all the evidence has been gathered. Despair always fails to remember that there is a whole lot more to God's plan for our lives than will ever be clear at one glance to your eyes or mine. That's why, at the height of your despair, you are least able to see the purpose that God is working out—steadily, unerringly—and true to God's loving plan for each of us.

While some persons might view despair as no more than a very disheartening aspect of burnout, the Christian can discover in many despairing situations opportunities for a new beginning. Such opportunities may be in the making even when you are despairing because your own dreams, hopes, and plans no longer hold much promise. Such despair, for example, often occurs to many married couples as each person tries to shape his or her own personal and vocational identity. Sharon Phelps, in her early thirties, was happily situated in the community where she, her husband, and their children lived. But her husband felt that he was at a dead end, vocationally, and needed to return to graduate school. Sharon was very disheartened and despairing when he shared the "good news" that he had been accepted at a university at the opposite end of the country. She had to decide if she wanted to pay the price to remain married to her husband. Sharon's despair was a clear indicator that her hopes for life to continue as it had for several years were no longer realistic. Despair forced her to face the reality that her life would have to change. There were new, promising chapters ahead of her, though at first they did not look very inviting.

The potential opportunity for moving beyond despair, as Sharon Phelps did, is also reflected in the journey of a young woman who broke her neck in a diving accident. (Joni Eareckson and Joe Musser, *Joni;* Bantam Books, 1978.) Joni, pronounced Johnny, had just graduated from high school and still had most of her life ahead of her when she was paralyzed from the neck down. The irony of Joni's accident was that she was left incapable of even the option of dealing with her despair *by taking her own life!*

Through the story, Joni explains how she struggled with her faith as she first denied the seriousness of her handicap and then realized how greatly limited her life would be. However, Joni also declares that she was able to find opportunities for her life that validated and affirmed her Christian faith. Gifted as an artist, Joni was able to develop a great skill in working with a pen she held in her teeth and has received national acclaim for her artwork. It is striking that in spite of the severity of her personal handicap, Joni is sincere in her exclamation that life still holds opportunity for her: "I really began to see suffering in a new light—not as trials to avoid, but as opportunities to 'grab,' because God gives so much of His love, grace, and goodness to those who do." (Eareckson and Musser, *Joni,* p. 157.)

"Opportunities to 'grab'" was obviously the approach of psychiatric nurse Darlene Raines, who cared for patients with long-term mental and medical problems. During one winter, a woman patient who was old and nearing death looked up at

Beyond Easy Answers 79

Darlene and said she wanted to see and feel the snow one more time. Darlene bundled the old woman up warmly and tightly, carried her outdoors, and held her while the woman smiled at the touch of the cold snow. Darlene had the spiritual sensitivity to recognize that it was simply an opportunity in a despairing situation to bring joy to a human heart.

Churches have those opportunities in the midst of despairing situations. Floyd Weber was pastor of a struggling downtown church. When Floyd left that church for another ministry opportunity, the congregation could not continue because there were not sufficient financial resources to call another pastor. The members despaired because they had worshiped together in the same location for many years. The congregation was dissolved and the building became a daycare center as part of a church-sponsored community outreach ministry. Floyd Weber's former church secretary wrote to him soon afterward: "You would not recognize the sanctuary since it has been remodeled. The rest rooms and toilets for the children are now located where the communion table used to be!" And is that not how it always is, God wresting an opportunity out of the clutches of despair, always doing it in ways that you and I would never have guessed or planned? The promise is that from God's viewpoint our despair shall never be the end of the story that God is writing for each of us!

Are You in Despair Now?

While you try to cope with your despair, you need to know that *your prayers are in themselves evidence that God is with you.* Ordinarily we think of prayer as being a long-distance telephone call. Often it seems to us that the line is busy or the operator disconnects us. Or, worse yet, there is an answer on the other end of the line, but then we are put on hold. Of course we feel frustrated and angered; we are in despair and God is not even available. Or so it seems.

The truth of the matter, however, is that prayer is not a long-distance telephone call. Rather, God is always present with us, and the question is always whether we are present with God. You and I are the ones who are usually absent or inattentive to God. It is not God who is inattentive to us! Again, the psalmist was unquestionably certain that God would be present in any condition or situation:

> If I ascend to heaven, thou art there!
> If I make my bed in Sheol, thou art there!
> If I take the wings of the morning
>   and dwell in the uttermost parts of the sea,
> even there thy hand shall lead me,
>   and thy right hand shall hold me.
> (Ps. 139:8–10)

When we pray we need to remember that God is present always through the act of creating us, through the love of Jesus Christ for us, and through the ever-present Spirit who helps us to pray because we do not even know how to pray. "Likewise the Spirit helps us in our weakness; for we do not know how to pray as we ought, but the Spirit himself intercedes for us with sighs too deep for words." (Rom. 8:26.) Our prayers are the prayers God has given us. God has already initiated the dialogue with us before we pray. Because we pray, we know the psalmist is correct; we cannot flee from God's presence, even if the darkness of despair covers us.

It is also important for you to remember *that God has given you the spiritual resources always to choose how you will face the future!* Regardless of the circumstances before you, you have a choice about your attitude, and you have a choice about your behavior and action. Just a couple of days ago I heard a woman complain to her husband, "You box me in when you say that!" It was important for her to realize she was boxing *herself* in. Despite how limited your options may be, nothing can take away the power God has given you for deciding how you will live with those options. Despair need never be your only spiritual option!

The biblical record shows that right from the beginning, if we take a good look at Adam and Eve, we have not often made good choices. Moses, however, called upon his brothers and sisters to make the right choices: "Therefore choose life, that you and your descendants may live, loving the LORD your God, obeying his voice, and cleaving to him" (Deut. 30:19b–20a). You can choose life by choosing attitudes and behaviors that are rooted in faith and hold the promise of hope.

Finally, *your life is still within the special purpose God has for you.* God still uses you and works through you even when you cannot figure out what good your life is. If there is not a beautiful purpose and potential in every human life, then why did Jesus so often leave the crowds and go over to the side of the road to touch and heal a leper or a blind beggar? What a seeming waste of time—except Jesus knew that in each of those obscure persons, unnoticed and passed over by everyone else, there was a wonderful purpose to be fulfilled in God's plan. Though we may be totally puzzled to understand how God can use our own or another's apparently useless life, we can only conclude that God's purposes for all human lives are usually beyond our very limited comprehension.

Your life matters greatly. The truth is that God has things to be done through your life that cannot be done through anyone else's life.

Things You Can Do

In the book of James you are reminded that the quality of a person's inner spiritual faith will be reflected in his or her outward behavior: "So faith by itself, if it has no works, is dead" (James 2:17). This spiritual truth about the link between your inner faith and your daily behavior will be particularly true as you cope with your despair. Your Christian hope and endurance may be well reflected in effective action if you:

1. Lift the blinds, let the light of day in, comb your hair, and get dressed.
2. Take time to be physically active and get some exercise besides the activity you get in your daily work.
3. Find a quiet time in your day for becoming aware of God's sustaining presence with you.
4. Pray with honesty, using words such as frustration, doubt, fear, and anger as well as joy, gratitude, and thanksgiving.
5. Eat regularly, maintain a nutritious diet, and get the sleep you need without staying in bed more than is necessary.
6. Connect with other people who will support you and love you.
7. Find a way to give love in something other than a romantic relationship.
8. Give yourself treats, like taking yourself out to dinner.
9. Be responsible for yourself and *immediately stop blaming* others or circumstances for your situation.
10. Seek professional help, through an experienced pastoral counselor or other mental health professional, when your despair continues to be endless and deepening.

The psalmist asks the question that most of us have prayed in our lowest hours, "Why are you cast down, O my soul, and why are you disquieted within me?" (Ps. 42:5a, 11a; 43:5a). Despair is a great burden upon the human heart, and it invariably accompanies the hopelessness that is characteristic of burnout. But despair does not separate you from God. You may feel estranged from God, but God's love and the presence of the Lord Jesus Christ are with you despite the continuing darkness of your journey. God remains faithful even when you are persuaded that there is no reason for hope or courage.

Wait upon the Lord, endure the struggle, and be renewed with the certain assurance that God's love and plan for you shall always be greater than your despair!

Chapter 5

In the Presence of Death

> Death is the supreme festival on the road to freedom.
> *Dietrich Bonhoeffer*
> Prisoner for God, *p. 176*
> Macmillan Co., 1961

> O death, where is thy victory?
> O death, where is thy sting?
> *I Corinthians 15:55*

The final question is death—our own and the death of those close to us. Death raises all the concerns about meaning, about God's existence, and about the purpose of life. Death dares us to make any sense of life; death challenges us to find any grounds for renewal and hope. Total spiritual, mental, and physical burnout can easily follow the realization that someone close to us or we ourselves will soon die. Likewise, the recent death of someone whom we love can make our own life very difficult to live with any sense of direction or purpose.

A life-threatening illness can suddenly change your whole purpose for living from hopefulness to despair. If I know that I am "terminally ill," what reason is there for living? I can no longer make plans with certainty or even think of the high school graduation of my tenth-grade daughter. Planning for a vacation next summer, which formerly had been anticipated six months in advance, may now be questionable. If I have cancer, I may have to live just one day at a time, because that is all the time I am permitted to enjoy. One can easily ask, "What's the use?"

It had been three years since his young wife's death, but Tom Reynolds still had little spirit for living and for his work. As we talked, it became very evident that Tom was still enraged at God because he felt that God had taken his wife so early in their marriage when they still had so many promising years ahead of them. Though he had an excellent job and many friends to support him, Tom just did not see how his life could be put back together without his wife. His wife's death had left Tom without any purpose or enthusiasm for living.

Thus, it is not surprising that you and I prefer to give little thought to death, even though the fact of death confronts us daily from our newspapers and our television screens. Ernest Becker has eloquently argued that we go to heroic lengths in our lives in order to avoid the fact that one day we shall die: "The idea of death, the fear of it, haunts the human animal like nothing else; it is a mainspring of human activity—activity designed largely to avoid the fatality of death, to overcome it by denying in some way that it is the final destiny for man [and woman]." (Ernest Becker, *The Denial of Death,* p. ix; Free Press, 1973.)

You and I know all too well the lengths we go to in order to avoid our own mortality. Going shopping and running our credit to its limit with plastic cards is a favorite way to avoid the truth about life, that there is a finality for each of us. In one way or another you and I build monuments which we hope will be a legacy that will transcend our brief experience of this life. Heroically, says Becker, we are establishing a career, writing a book, investing our assets, and building institutions, all with the hope that somehow our efforts to leave something of ourselves behind will cheat death of having the final word.

The Reality and the Hope

There is much evidence that the Bible takes death very seriously. Certainly the writer of Ecclesiastes counted death as one of the elemental passages of life.

> For everything there is a season, and a time for every matter under heaven:
> a time to be born, and a time to die.
> (Eccl. 3:1–2a)

The New Testament goes even further by saying that God has become very personally involved with death for our sake. If indeed Jesus had not died on a cross, there would have been no gospel. Everything that the gospel means for salvation and eternal life for all of God's people comes to sharp focus and turns upon the tragedy of the Son of God abandoned in death at Golgotha.

The purpose of the New Testament to come to grips with the awesome and terrifying reality of death is poignantly gathered up in Luke's words that convey Jesus' resolute intention to make his final journey into Jerusalem.

> When the days drew near for him to be received up, he set his face to go to Jerusalem. (Luke 9:51)

There was to be no turning back; the stage was set for Jesus not just to challenge the religious and civil authorities but also to confront all the authority of death itself.

The gospel stands face to face and toe to toe with the final reality of death. When God's love was set on that cross for all the world to see, there was no drinking, drugging, or shopping in order to avoid the facts that you and I wish would just go away!

Elie Wiesel, survivor of Auschwitz and the murder of six million Jews, has recalled that fellow prisoners asked each other where God was while they watched the murder of their

In the Presence of Death

comrades. Wiesel heard himself answer in his own heart that God was there hanging on the gallows with the victims, enduring the agony of their own slow death. (Elie Wiesel, *Night,* 1969, pp. 75f.; cited by Jürgen Moltmann, *The Crucified God,* pp. 273–274; Harper & Row, 1974.)

The Christian has no difficulty seeing the Christ there suffering and dying on every gallows. That is the meaning of the cross. God himself is there where every human being must face and die a godforsaken death. Death is the place of the great encounter with the God who died at Golgotha and who suffers with all God's people who are dying. Death is the great encounter with the power and the love of the crucified Christ himself. Death is the great encounter with the Christ who, as Lord of life, completes death with the resurrection that gives an everlasting hope.

The power of that resurrection has been evident to me in the lives of many people whom I have known as a pastor who have had to face their own imminent death or the death of a loved one. Certainly people always experience many wide-ranging emotions about their own death or the death of someone close to them. Of course there are the feelings of shock, grief, anger, rage, and guilt. Some people may weep openly, while others keep their feelings behind a well-composed face. All those feelings and reactions are real and natural. And just as real and true are the words that tell us who it is that transcends death, the words that tell us whom we shall always belong to: "I am the resurrection and the life; he who believes in me, though he die, yet shall he live, and whoever lives and believes in me shall never die" (John 11:25–26a).

When Christians gather for the funeral of a friend or family member, and when they walk with the casket to the gravesite, they rightfully call that occasion a "witness to the resurrection." Though human emotions may not be able to focus or grasp the resurrection reality at such a moment, there is still One who transcends what appears to us to be the end of life.

Even in the lives of those who are not professed Christians, there is clear evidence of the Christ's resurrection hope. The story of Anne Frank tells of a Jewish family in hiding from the Nazis from July 6, 1942, till their secret living quarters were found August 4, 1944. Though Anne wrote that she could hear the approaching thunder that would destroy her, she affirmed that she could look up into the heavens and know that the cruelty would end and that peace and tranquillity would return once again. (Anne Frank, *The Diary of a Young Girl,* p. 287; Doubleday & Co., 1967.) In the face of the imminent darkness, Anne saw a new heaven and a new earth. And the Christian knows who the Author of such a vision must be!

For it is in the face of death that you and I discover the difference between what is lasting reality and what no longer matters. Jesus Christ offers the comfort that helps us to see what is real and worthy of our attention. It is just like the final scene in Dickens' *A Tale of Two Cities.* Sidney Carton and the young woman are bound and standing in line, waiting their turn to mount the gallows and bow before the guillotine. While the crowd yells after each thudding death blow of the executioner's machine, Carton reassures his companion and steadies her with these words: "Keep your eyes upon me, dear child, and mind no other object." (Charles Dickens, *A Tale of Two Cities,* p. 375; New American Library of World Literature, 1960.) In the presence of death, we who affirm Christ as Lord are called to mind no other object but him who died and rose again so you and I never have to stop living!

What then do we as modern Christians say about death? We have no doubt that others die and that we, too, shall die. We know as well as the writer of Ecclesiastes that "all go to one place; all are from the dust, and all turn to dust again" (Eccl. 3:20). Indeed, we do not need researchers to remind us that ultimately the body does not have the physiological capacity to survive the stresses of this life. Though the spirit of the person in the body may remain very young, the body's aging process continues its relentless pace. Many persons who are young enough in spirit to want to enjoy climbing mountains or sailing over rolling waters find themselves confined and restricted by disintegrating vertebrae, crippling arthritis, failing sight, and diseased hearts.

One would think that the sheer knowledge alone that all shall die should be the ultimate stressor that makes life pointless. So why do you and I continue to go on living? Why do we get out of bed day after day? There is no logical reason for living, for bearing children, for paying off the mortgage on your house, and for putting your children through college. The writer in Ecclesiastes is certainly correct with the repeated solemn observation that "all is vanity."

Then, in view of all the overwhelming evidence that tells us life ends with death, how on earth do we account for the fact that you and I do get out of bed; we do bear children and send them through college; we do, much of the time, live with hope, and purpose, and with a yearning to make our lives count? Is Ernest Becker's explanation sufficient that the reason you and I live with purpose is that somehow we think we can defeat death by leaving something behind that will outlast us? No, it seems very unlikely that people who know they shall die can generate from within themselves their own vital hope, particularly a convincing hope that can keep them living a full lifetime.

The obvious conclusion is that hope in the face of death does not spring from us humans! The gifts of hope, courage, and endurance, which dare to keep on living despite the awesomeness of death, are not something you and I manage because we grit our teeth, clench our fists, and try a little harder to crank up some believable hope. The courage to live, which is in most persons, is God's creation and God's gift. The power we Christians joyously bear witness to as the Resurrection is the same power that renews all human flesh from one moment to the next. God is love, and God is life!

And it is the joy of the Christian faith to celebrate and to serve the Giver of such life!

So, as overwhelming as all the evidence is that you and I shall die, even more persuasive and empowering is the fact of life itself! And those of us who call ourselves Christians simply want the rest of the world to know that we have seen the Author and the Giver of that life. Not only have we seen him, but we want all to know that he has raised up an empty cross over every human life as the steady, unswerving sign that *death shall never be the purpose or the end of our days!*

Such an affirmation takes on a deeper perspective when viewed against the backdrop of a prisoner-of-war camp where death can be seen or smelled or touched in almost any direction one cares to turn. Ernest Gordon, former dean of the chapel at Princeton University, has described such an experience in his book *Through the Valley of the Kwai*. Gordon recounts his experience as one of the sixty thousand prisoners of war who were forced to build a railroad along the Kwai River for several hundred miles. The toll in human lives paid for the building of that railroad earned it the appropriate label Railroad of Death. Part of the inhuman task faced by the prisoners of war working on the railroad was the building of the now infamous bridge over the Kwai River.

Gordon tells of his own skepticism about the Christian faith, a skepticism that was reinforced as he saw men regressing to meanness and living like animals with little or no thought or concern for their fellow prisoners. But what Gordon describes as a miracle took place as a new spirit of caring began to return to the prisoners. For Gordon, his own eyes were opened by the generous behavior of two men who carefully and patiently nursed him back from death. Likewise, Gordon could not forget the selfless and courageous attitudes of two particular men who were executed by their captors for performing acts of mercy for their fellow prisoners. The spirit of faith and generosity began unmistakably to arise and change the prison camp. Gordon found himself, to his

In the Presence of Death

surprise, in the midst of men who were discovering the power of their Christian faith to face their unrelenting companion, death. As Gordon and his friends gathered to read the Bible and to discuss their faith, a clear, emerging vision of Jesus came to them.

> True, he had been strung up on a cross and tormented with the hell of pain; but he had not broken. The weight of law and of prejudice had borne down on him but failed to crush him. He had remained free and alive, as the resurrection affirmed. What he was, what he did, what he said, all made sense for us. (Ernest Gordon, *Through the Valley of the Kwai*, p. 138; Harper & Row, 1962)

The miracle for Gordon was that in the midst of the death camp in which he lived he was finally able to affirm to himself and to those about him: "Reason said, 'We live to die.' Jesus said, 'I am the resurrection and the life.' " (Gordon, *Through the Valley of the Kwai*, p. 139.)

Many persons would say that the worst way to have to deal with death is to endure the death of a loved one. There is no greater stress than to lose one's spouse or a child. The life adjustments that must be made following such a death can be overwhelming. There are many persons who continue to grieve over their loss for many years. Everything within one's soul and being will resist the awful fact that one so close to you is gone. I can still vividly remember being called, not many years ago, in the middle of the night. Bill Thompson was only forty-seven and seemingly in good health. Tuesday morning he was rushed to the hospital with a massive heart attack. His wife, Lois, was advised Wednesday morning that despite Bill's critical condition, he had stabilized. But late Wednesday evening I received the call from friends staying with Lois. The hospital had just called to say Bill had had another heart attack and all attempts to revive him had failed.

I went immediately to Lois' home, and I shall never forget her devastating grief; she was still in shock at the news of her husband's death. Physically she reacted by involuntary retching and vomiting, as if her body wanted to expel the terrible reality that had just descended upon her.

Even in the face of such a horrible shock, God's love still endures and stands tall like an empty cross that refuses to be swept away by all our sorrow. James Angell, a Presbyterian minister, has written a sensitive and beautiful account of how he and his family lived through the hours and the days following the accidental death of their twenty-one-year-old daughter, Susan, who fell asleep while driving home the Saturday night before Easter. James was the one to answer the telephone and receive the message from the sheriff's office. Then he repeated the terrible words to his wife, "Susan's been killed in an accident." At that point, he writes, "The world fell off its axis." (James W. Angell, *O Susan!*, p. 13; Warner Press, 1973.)

James Angell preached the Easter sermon, only a few hours later, which he had already prepared. With the pain of his daughter's death tearing at his own soul, he told his parishioners that morning:

> Easter is the gift of life because it is the gift of seeing, the power to hope, the will to believe that beyond death is God and life and that our lives are mortgaged to both of these truths. (Angell, *O Susan!*, p. 95)

You cannot live this life without the ever-present threat of death, no matter how protected and sheltered you may be in our American culture. Though we are vaccinated by our way of living against most catastrophic forms of death that take so much human life elsewhere around the world, still there is hardly a family that is not dealing with death or the advancing threat of death. And how do we cope? Surely not by our own resources. Not one of us is equal to the task. Rather, the One

In the Presence of Death

who could not be confined by death to a tomb invites us to claim all the promise of his Easter. And who can resist such an invitation?

Life-Threatening Illness

Despite the medical advances that have been made in the treatment of cancer, receiving a diagnosis that a person has one of the various forms of cancer is very frightening for many people and certainly life-changing for most. The discovery of cancer within oneself or within a loved one or friend certainly causes most people to face the ultimate questions about the purpose and meaning of life.

Of course you do not have to be a Christian in order to cope with cancer or to be successfully treated for cancer. Nor by any means does being a Christian ensure that one will not experience cancer or have a remission or cure of one's cancer. But most surely the various resources of the Christian faith enable many to deal with the anxieties, the uncertainties, the exhaustion, and the pain that can be associated with one's experience of cancer as a patient or as a family member. Cancer can bring the widest range of emotional experiences, from profound despair to rage to guilt and relentless self-pity. The Christian faith does not promise protection from those discouraging feelings, just as the Christian faith does not promise to keep you or a loved one from having cancer. The Christian faith promises more, a Presence that knows death firsthand, a Presence that does not flee even when you are filled with doubt, a Presence that is always bidding and inviting you never to stop living—now and always!

Do not take your anger about a life-threatening illness as meaning that you have no faith. Even your anger with God does not mean that you have lost your faith. I have talked with numerous cancer patients who were glad to talk with me until they discovered that I was a minister. Then suddenly they became uncomfortable and abruptly ended the conversa tion. A couple of them explained that my being a minister forced them to deal with God more than they were ready to do. They were angry, but that does not mean they were far from God. God is always present, even if we are angry, which suggests that certainly our anger can be a vital form of prayer!

A minister wrote to me about his angry feelings when his wife was recently diagnosed as having cancer.

> This is strictly honest. Part of my hostility arises from my anger and rebellion to have cancer come to the one I love the most. For a long time, over thirty years, I have tried to minister to those who have unexpected illnesses come to them or their loved ones.
>
> The terror of my first reaction to think I might be separated from my wife was unthinkable. The faith I have talked about for so long came to bear on my plight. "The Lord is my shepherd, I shall not want ... " actually became my stay and strength. I do not know how to measure stress; all I can say is that we have had a great deal of stress with this cancer, and I believe our faith is an essential tool for recovery and hope when the feelings of terror are so strong.

As I have listened to how cancer patients cope with the stress created by their illness, I have heard five consistent themes from most of them. First of all, prayer is unquestionably a major source of help. Somehow, in the midst of their health crisis, many persons often find that they are able to carry on a conversation with God that is more natural and honest for them than before their illness. Less than a year ago Susan Potter was diagnosed as having a form of cancer that left her with much pain and fatigue. Also, it has been difficult for her to move about, and she has had to remain in bed for long periods of time. Nonetheless, the presence of God was never in doubt for her, and she and God often have very intimate conversations. She explains:

> I would say to God, "You're going to have to push if I am going to make it out of bed." I went through a period of being very angry with God for six or eight weeks. I didn't want to talk with God at all then. Now I talk to him at night, and I just say to him, "I'm really down." I tell him, "Come on, you've got to help me." I don't get on my knees. I just say to him, "Come on now, don't let me down."

Second, such persons consistently talk about the magnificent support and love they have experienced from family, friends, and church members. The knowledge that dozens, even hundreds, of people are praying for them provides indescribable support when facing surgery and long days of uncertainty. Pat Swanson in particular told me how grateful she was for the loving support she experienced as she waited in the hospital for the results from tests that would show how far the cancer had spread in her body. Her minister told her he would be reporting to the congregation, during the time for parish prayers and concerns in the worship service, that Pat was hospitalized. Pat exclaimed:

> It meant so much to me just knowing that others in the church knew about my hospitalization. I was surprised that I felt so much strength because I knew that so many people were praying for me and thinking about me. Now I pray much more often for others, because I know it meant so much to me.

Pat had experienced the power, love, and support that is so characteristic of the body of Christ, the fellowship of the church. That fellowship is a vital and undergirding source of strength for the Christian dealing with the stress and uncertainty of serious illness.

Third, most people who have cancer or any other kind of life-threatening illness usually speak of their deep gratitude for the simple things of life, the beauty of the present day, and their newly discovered relationships with people. Now they really want to take the time to linger over the sounds, smells, and sights that before they were somehow too busy to notice. Jesus often invited his friends and disciples to notice the things you and I are usually too preoccupied to see: the lilies of the field, a sparrow, the little children, a poor widow, a blind man beside the road. To have our eyes and ears opened so we begin to see life once again is God's special grace and gift!

For one cancer patient the gift of deepened awareness brought the rediscovery of the importance of friends.

> I was a person who hurried a lot. But all that hurrying was really just indifference to giving any thought to the direction of my life. Friends are so important to me now. I hadn't, before, spent enough time developing those friendships.

Then that person added:

> My faith has helped me to accept the things I cannot change. I don't understand why so many things happen. I don't know the plan; nonetheless, I do the best I can each day, and one day I'll know where I fit in the plan.
>
> In the meantime, some little things are no longer as important as I used to think. I find that I am more sensitive now to the birds and the trees.

Likewise, Roger Snyder does not believe that God gave him cancer, but he does believe that through his cancer his spiritual life has been deepened considerably. Now life has greater meaning for him and he cares for people more than he did before his illness.

> Cancer has accelerated my sense of purpose. It's a joy to go to a wedding. When I was first diagnosed with cancer I was very angry. Now I am much more service oriented, especially in the volunteer hospice program visiting terminally ill patients.

Fourth, it is evident that many cancer patients are strengthened by a lively sense of hope. Mary Harper recalled her husband's death and the courage he showed only six weeks before he died with cancer. On the way to the hospital, he told Mary, "We have to believe that God sees beyond where we see." Although most cancer patients remain realistic about their illness, that does not prevent them from looking ahead with much anticipation for life. Instead of planning mindlessly five and ten years ahead, they have a focused sense of hope that values the coming weeks and months. One cancer patient spoke of faith and hope in these terms:

> I have learned that life's difficulties depend upon my attitude. It depends on us whether we emerge through a crisis stronger, weaker, or more vulnerable. I have a profound faith in God, and I know that because of God I am here and whole.
>
> I think of death as a beginning. This present life is a preparation for me. The agony will someday be in giving up people here that I love. But the excitement is that through death I will be coming to a fulfillment of my journey. All things considered, cancer is a minor crisis in my life.
>
> I've tried to walk in my valleys with dignity so I can stand on my hills with pride!

Such hope is at the very heart of the Christian affirmation that God is love, God is life!

Fifth, cancer patients who report that their faith has been a valuable source of help for them also usually describe various activities they are engaged in so they can help others. More than ten years ago Rita Benson had a hysterectomy for a malignant tumor, and three years later a mastectomy. Then her husband was diagnosed as having cancer. He died three years later. Rita has repeatedly asked herself why it has been she who has survived. Free of cancer now for nine years, Rita says:

> Looking back, I can see that through my faith in God there has always been something for me to

hold on to. At times my faith wavered as I asked myself "Why am I here?" Without my faith it would have been so much harder to survive. I guess I am here to help others if I can do it. Now I do volunteer work for the Cancer Society, and I visit others who are being treated for cancer. Now I can help others, which seems the purpose for my having had cancer.

Though their awareness of the immediacy of death has been heightened by their illness, it is evident that many cancer patients are relying upon their Christian faith resources for coping and living beyond hopelessness and spiritual burnout. As an example, Lucy Miller found herself very anxious about the possibility that the changes she had noted in her body could indicate cancer. However, once that diagnosis was confirmed, she could accept the seriousness of her illness while relying upon the support, prayers, and concern of many friends in her church. Lucy coped with her infrequent despondency by trying not to dwell on the question, "Why me?" Moreover, the words in I Thessalonians 5:18a, "give thanks in all circumstances," began to help her see her illness in a new perspective. She was especially thankful for her body's response to the chemotherapy and for the loving attention of so many people close to her. As Lucy drew upon her Christian faith as her primary resource in coping with her illness, she was able to affirm: "I just feel fortunate to have many healing blessings and to have had so much wonderful strength and health through all the years. I praise God continually for what he has done for me and my spouse, who has cared for me so well."

The Christian faith calls you and me to practice the spiritual values that many cancer patients are discovering firsthand in the midst of their health crisis. We *can* live despite whatever situation or condition we find ourselves in. We need not live with our eyes closed and teeth clenched as if life were just one swallow of bitter medicine after another. Even with the

In the Presence of Death

unnerving shock of a life-threatening illness, the Christ still offers us the experience of life which can only be called "abundant." And that is a fact that has been discovered and verified by so many!

Though not by intention, somehow it worked out that I am completing this chapter on Easter Day. As in most of our churches this triumphant day, the service of worship at Presbyterian Church of the Way in Shoreview, Minnesota, began with these words:

LEADER: Christ is risen!
PEOPLE: **He is risen indeed!**
LEADER: Our God has triumphed over death and the grave.
PEOPLE: **Praise God! Christ is risen: Hallelujah!**

Later in the service we heard this good news:

But in fact Christ has been raised from the dead, the first fruits of those who have fallen asleep. For as by a man came death, by a man has come also the resurrection of the dead. For as in Adam all die, so also in Christ shall all be made alive. (I Cor. 15:20–22)

The Scripture readings were followed with a sermon by the pastor, Neal E. Lloyd, appropriately entitled "Real Grave—Real Victory." The service of worship concluded as we sang:

The day of resurrection!
Earth, tell it out abroad!
The Passover of gladness,
The Passover of God!
From death to life eternal,
From this world to the sky,
Our Christ has brought us over
With hymns of victory.
("The Day of Resurrection!"
The Worshipbook, p. 584)

Thomas C. Campbell was the former academic vice-president of the United Theological Seminary in New Brighton,

Minnesota. Widely recognized as a scholar and a churchman, Tom was beloved by all who knew him and were associated with him in his work as a seminary educator and administrator. On January 28, 1979, surgery revealed a malignant tumor, and Tom died from the cancer on August 12, 1979. On February 12, shortly after the surgery and diagnosis of his cancer, Tom included these words in an open letter to the seminary community:

> Some new word-concept combinations have moved to "center stage" from being only in the supporting cast, words like: confidence with caution, dreading but daring, celebrating uncertainty, combining hope and realism, and learning when to be happily dependent and when to be an *active* agent in the healing process.
>
> None of us ever know how God's graciousness and love will next be revealed to us, but I can close for now by telling you that when Paul wrote the last nine verses of his eighth chapter to the Christians at Rome, *he knew what he was talking about and he is right!* (*Monday Morning at UTS*, III-2-78/79, p. 3; used by permission of Donna Campbell)

The confident witness of Tom Campbell and so many others confirms that even in the presence of death we shall, by God's incomprehensible grace, mount up with wings like eagles, run and not be weary, walk and not faint (Isa. 40:31). That promise is not a promise that you shall not become ill or that you shall not lose those who are close to you. That promise is not a promise that you shall never walk through your own valley of the shadow of death. Rather, the promise is that when you walk through that valley you shall not be alone, and all the way through even out to the other side there is always life—rich, deep, and abundant. And we have that promise on the highest authority!

There is life beyond our burnout, even the burnout that comes with death!

Chapter 6

Your Neighbor as Yourself

> "Lord, when did we see thee hungry and feed thee, or thirsty and give thee drink? And when did we see thee a stranger and welcome thee, or naked and clothe thee? And when did we see thee sick or in prison and visit thee?" And the King will answer them, "Truly, I say to you, as you did it to one of the least of these my brethren, you did it to me."
>
> *Matthew 25:37b–40*

> Strangely enough I don't feel stressed when I'm helping other people in a stressful situation.
>
> *The comment of a layperson after teaching a Vietnamese refugee how to drive a car*

The principal resource to the Christian for coping with stress is Jesus Christ himself. He promises us that you and I shall find him when we are responding to the needs of other persons. As Christians we cannot give consideration to our own personal stress alone without also having deep concern for, and involvement with, the problems, issues, and forces that create burdening stress for our neighbor, whoever in the world that person might be.

It is true that responsible Christian living requires the new priority of taking very good care of ourselves, our personal, mental, physical, and spiritual resources. But too easily you and I often slip into an either/or mentality about our spiritual responsibilities. We lose a sense of spiritual balance and perspective when we focus on caring only for others, or caring only for ourselves. We know very well that Jesus asks you and me to "love your neighbor as yourself," which is a spiritual commandment that has its roots deep in our Judeo-Christian heritage (Lev. 19:18; Matt. 22:39). Our spiritual balance will have an appropriate perspective only when we love both our neighbor and ourself. As Jesus made clear, such a spiritual goal can be possible only if we first love God, and if we are strengthened and renewed by God's grace.

Self-preoccupation is not the same as self-care. While responsible self-care is attentive to one's own needs as a whole person, self-preoccupation usually ends up distorting and magnifying one's needs. Adolescent behavior, for example, while appropriate to teenagers often reflects much self-preoccupation. The typical thirteen-, fourteen-, or fifteen-year-old regularly stands in front of a mirror and takes painstaking care to make certain every hair is exactly in its correct position. Such self-preoccupation occurs repeatedly despite little concern for the appearance of the teenager's bedroom, which usually looks like a disaster area. Such self-preoccupation, however, has its place in early human development, but it certainly has no place in adult behavior. Invariably, adult self-preoccupation in most persons leads to much miserableness and unhappiness. Self-preoccupation will only increase stress and burnout for you and me, never lessen it.

We are called to balance our spiritual perspective, to love our neighbor as ourself, in a world that daily is rapidly redefining the notion of who our neighbor is. Writer John Naisbitt informs us that when President Lincoln was assassinated, the news was communicated throughout our country by telegraph. But because there were no direct wire linkups with England, it took five days for the news to reach London. By contrast, when President Reagan was shot, journalist Henry Fairlie, working at his desk within a block from the shooting, received word of the event by telephone from his editor in London, who had seen a rerun of the assassination attempt on television only moments after it took place! (John Naisbitt, *Megatrends: Ten New Directions Transforming Our Lives*, p. 23; Warner Books, 1982.) Because of the electronic age in which we live and the technology that places communication satellites in orbit over our heads, virtually the whole world now is as near as your backyard and mine!

Lee and Betty McClain are typical of the increasing number of Christians who feel very deeply that they live in a worldwide community of neighbors. Moreover, their conviction about living in a responsible relationship with all persons is also linked to how they cope with the personal dimensions of their own stress and burnout. For example, one of the most difficult times in Betty's life occurred right after they were married and they had to move to a new community because of Lee's work. Betty remembers how she struggled with loneliness, as she found herself home alone most of the day in a new community where she did not know anyone.

Lee and Betty began attending a church shortly after moving to the new community. Still struggling with her intense loneliness, Betty reached an important conclusion about two months after beginning to attend the new church. She realized that while sitting in church she was hearing about the many concerns other people had, such as family members being in the hospital or near death. Then Betty explained: "I remember thinking that what I needed to do was get out and go do something to help some of those people who had real problems—problems far greater than mine! I realized that by getting involved with other people's problems I would be taking care of my own loneliness!"

Lee described an earlier time when he was wrestling within himself to find some meaning and reason for his life. He really wondered if there was any useful purpose he could find; his life seemed so pointless to him. His inner searching was intensified by health problems and chronic fatigue, which left him feeling depressed, helpless, and unimportant. He was not managing the stress in his life well at all. There were no flashes of brilliant or instant insight for Lee, but in time he came to some important conclusions about the sources of much of his stress. Lee discovered that he could not find the answers he was looking for by focusing only on himself. He found his fulfillment when his attention also included others' needs. Moreover, he adds, "Today when I think things are going bad for me I can look around at what's going on for others, and it certainly makes the burden much easier to bear."

Over the years Lee and Betty have become quite involved in their identification and concern with the needs of others. They have worked side by side with blacks and whites in an educational tutoring program. They also gave leadership to a biracial discussion group when identification with such a group was not popular in their community. In another city they provided time and effort to a ministry for poor, elderly residents.

When you talk with people like Lee and Betty, who are giving several hours each month to invest in others' lives, you usually discover you are talking with a person who has a radiant spirit as well as a steady confidence for handling stress. Loving others with your time and your energy somehow invariably stimulates your own spiritual renewal and increases your resources for coping with your own stress.

Living in a country where being overweight is one of the major public health problems, and this in a world where countless thousands of persons are always starving to death, how can we American Christians think only about our own stress? The gospel requires us to ask that question and many other similar questions. How many people in this world even need the luxury of a book on stress management when their first essential is to have enough food to feed the children who lie in front of them starving to death? And what if, in a moment of collective madness, humanity should blow itself up in a cataclysmic nuclear exchange between the superpowers? What use then would all our talk about stress management have been? Who needs stress management techniques and resources after they have just been vaporized or their body burned beyond recognition by radiation? Somehow, those questions about critical worldwide issues just cannot be avoided when Christians begin to consider how to cope with the stress in their own lives.

Stressful Facts That Need Management

Many of us live in suburbia, where it is easy to pretend the rest of the world does not exist. Even though our television screen gives us a front-row view in our own family room of what is happening worldwide, still the life-style of middle-class America easily insulates many of us from the disturbing, stressful facts about how most of the rest of the people in the world are living. Many Christians in our country live in neighborhoods where the poverty level would begin at about $20,000 a year for a family of four. Survival at that level, of course, requires having two cars, a canoe or camper, two television sets, and perhaps even a home computer! This is not to mention the necessity of having a charcoal grill on the deck and a fertilizer spreader, to make certain the lawn grows sufficiently so there is reason to mow it every Saturday with one's gasoline-powered mower. No wonder it is difficult for you and me to grasp what it means for a family of four on the other side of the world to have only $150 a year to survive on!

Life-style assessment resources are available to help middle-class Christians like you and me begin to grapple with the implications of how our neighbors in the rest of the world are living. If you decide to take seriously the Christian ramifications of how you live, you are faced with "a fundamental challenge to the American pursuit of the good life in terms of material success and material consumption. For the church, lifestyle becomes a major question of Christian faithfulness at the beginning of a new era in history." (William E. Gibson, *A Covenant Group for Lifestyle Assessment: Participant's Manual*, p. 4; Program Agency, The United Presbyterian Church U.S.A., 1978.)

If you and I are seriously going to compare our life-style with that of our neighbors, we need to be aware that many developing countries must meet the demands of widespread population growth with fewer resources than do developed countries with smaller populations. The developing countries (including Africa and Latin America) have had only 88 percent of the food required properly to nourish their citizens, while the developed countries (including North America) had 130 percent. (Hana Umlauf Lane, ed., *The World Almanac and Book of Facts: 1983*, p. 166; Newspaper Enterprise Association, 1981.) An equally dramatic illustration of the imbalance of resources is the fact that Asia has 60 percent of the world's estimated population and only 30 percent of the world's land area. Meanwhile, North America has only 8 percent of the world's estimated population and 16 percent of the world's land area. (Ibid., p. 599.)

The greatest imbalance and injustice in this world, of course, is the difference between what the nations spend to prepare for war or to maintain wars and what is spent on food, medicine, and housing. Former professor of New Testament literature and exegesis J. Carter Swaim has drawn to our attention the great disparity between the money going for war in our world and the funds being directed to the essentials for human survival. Swaim declares that the world is spending well over *$1 billion every day* in preparation for war, while only approximately $17 billion *a year* would be required to provide adequate food, water, education, health care, and housing for everyone in the world. (J. Carter Swaim, *War, Peace, and the Bible*, p. 91; Orbis Books, 1982; citing *Development Forum*, Jan.–Feb. 1980, p. 8.) Swaim is certainly correct when he asserts, "It was never envisaged that on God's good earth there would be occasion for people to slaughter their brethren." (Swaim, *War, Peace, and the Bible,* p. 90.)

Despite the facts about food and war that are at least somewhat familiar to most of us, the greatest spiritual problem and fact of our day is *indifference.* How else do you account for the difficulty so many of us have in grasping the urgency of what is happening throughout the world, and the reluctance we have to make ourselves involved in such a way that we will not be part of the problem but part of the solution? Jesus was talking about such indifference when he told the story about the man beaten by robbers on the road that led from Jerusalem down to Jericho. (Luke 10:29–37.) In that story, some very good people passed by on the other side of the road, ignoring the man lying half-dead in the ditch. No doubt the priest and the Levite had good reasons for not troubling themselves; good people usually do have such good reasons when they are busy and have a lot of things on their mind.

Perhaps our spiritual indifference is caused in part by the enormity of the problem facing the world and confronting each one of us. Many of us know, if we give it any thought, that we live, sleep, go to work, and rear our families in a bull's-eye on the map of a military planner on the other side of the world. That fact is the same as living twenty-four hours a day with a loaded gun pointed at your head! For our own sanity we often choose to pretend such incomprehensible and such personally devastating facts are not true. Indeed, it takes great courage to recognize the gravity of the situation in which we live. It takes a determined spiritual resolve to deal with the assessment of an informed person such as retired Admiral Hyman G. Rickover, when he said: "The U.S.-Soviet arms race is so wildly out of control that instead of increasing our capacity to defend ourselves we are more likely to wipe out the human race in nuclear war. . . . I think probably we will destroy ourselves." (Quoted by Ronald J. Sider and Richard K. Taylor, *Nuclear Holocaust and Christian Hope,* p. 293; Paulist Press, 1982.)

Our spiritual indifference to the crisis facing ourselves and our neighbors in the world is reinforced certainly by the myth, "Whatever I might do will make no difference." The problems of worldwide food distribution and the control of nuclear arms are so enormous, and the billions of dollars involved so great, that each individual is easily left with the conclusion there is nothing one person can do that would make any difference. Clara Barton first worked unnoticed and unknown to most people as a schoolteacher and a clerk in the U.S. Patent Office before going out to the battlefields of the Civil War to bring aid to the wounded and the dying. Later she established the American Red Cross and was its first president for over twenty years. But unlike Clara Barton, most of us will not be the founders of an organization that will greatly benefit humankind. No, whatever you and I do will probably not gain much widespread attention if we choose to put some of our life's effort toward helping our neighbor.

All that can be said is to make the observation that Jesus never offered his disciples a yardstick for taking a daily reading on how much they had accomplished. In fact, the kinds of measuring standards Jesus usually talked about have a way of turning upside down how you and I like to measure things. For example, the poor widow who gave only two copper coins was giving more than anyone else; those who think they are first shall be last; and whoever would be great among the disciples would be their servant. So, we Christians are not to be too troubled about measuring whether or not we are making a significant contribution toward helping our neighbor. Rather, the point seems to be whether we are doing anything at all, and how much of our generous resources we are committing to the enterprise.

There are very stressful facts that need management in our world today, and we as Christians cannot justify our continued avoidance of those facts. Robert McAfee Brown has asserted that the facts are so stark they can hardly be comprehended, but they still remain true: "Fifteen thousand people starving to death every day, two thirds of the human family going to bed hungry every night. We cannot ignore those realities, since they are not statistics but people." (Robert McAfee Brown, *Making Peace in the Global Village*, p. 76; Westminster Press, 1981.)

Though you and I certainly have no intention of being violent persons, our affluent life-style is experienced as violence by others when their children have bloated stomachs from malnutrition and starve to death before their eyes. You and I may be moved by sympathy for the enormity of the human tragedy, or we may simply become anxious enough to do something because we know a catastrophic war could easily occur when there is such a great disparity between the haves and the have-nots. Whatever it is that gets your attention and mine, we can no longer live so naively in our provincial middle-class existence. Nothing in our Christian faith can permit us to be concerned only about the problems of our own personal stress while ignoring our brothers and sisters and their children, who are the victims of where they were born, the victims of political injustice and oppression, the victims of a world that values margins of profit more highly than margins of survival for human life.

Living as World Citizens

The spiritual theme of this chapter can be put this way: *as you and I enlarge our capacity for loving others, we shall see more of our own problems in their proper and less stressful perspective.* Another way to put that important theme is to take a walk where Jesus continually walks and measure your problems against the problems of those with whom he associates. Then you have the opportunity to place your problems side by side with those who are dying of malnutrition, suffering cruel imprisonment, being uprooted by the horrors of war, or living with permanent illness that is continually painful and crippling. A lot of one's problems can look pretty insignificant against such a list as that. Loving your neighbor as yourself is not only what Jesus has asked us clearly to do, it most certainly is also one of the best ways to begin handling one's own stress much more effectively.

Increasingly, more Christians are lifting their spiritual eyes and concerns to broader horizons. One such group of persons, persuaded that their faith required a worldwide vision of who their neighbor is, drew up a life-style covenant that reflected their conviction that their responsibilities were related to the needs of the whole world. Thus they asserted their intention to do something about such world-sized problems as pollution, nuclear armaments, economic injustice, discrimination, and the denial of human rights. This is the covenant they agreed to follow:

> Recognizing that the earth and the fullness thereof is a gift from our gracious God, and that we are called to cherish, nurture, and provide loving stewardship for the earth's resources, and recognizing that life itself is a gift, and a call to responsibility, joy, and celebration, I make the following declarations:
> 1. I declare myself to be a world citizen.
> 2. I commit myself to lead an ecologically sound life.
> 3. I commit myself to lead a life of creative simplicity and to share my personal wealth with the world's poor.
> 4. I commit myself to join with others in the reshaping of institutions in order to bring about a more just global society in which all people have full access to the needed resources for their physical, emotional, intellectual, and spiritual growth.
> 5. I commit myself to occupational accountability, and in so doing I will seek to avoid the creation of products which cause harm to others.

6. I affirm the gift of my body, and commit myself to its proper nourishment and physical well-being.
7. I commit myself to examine continually my relations with others, and to attempt to relate honestly, morally, and lovingly to those around me.
8. I commit myself to personal renewal through prayer, meditation, and study.
9. I commit myself to responsible participation in a community of faith.

(Adam Daniel Corson-Finnerty, *World Citizen: Action for Global Justice*, pp. 5–6; Orbis Books, 1982)

This covenant outlines one way of taking seriously the fact that we live in a global village and that being Christians in that village will not permit us to be indifferent. Persons with a biblical view of their own life and the world about them can no longer be unconcerned, particularly when the sources of stress overwhelming most other people are so much greater than the stress most of us put up with in our own lives. The moral imperative rooted in our biblical and Christian traditions is unmistakable. Jack Nelson draws our attention to the essential point when he asserts, "If God's love is the starting point of faith, the condition of our neighbor is the yardstick by which we judge the effectiveness of our love and the authenticity of our faith." Nelson then underscores the fact that love in the biblical sense is more than just how much feeling we have about our faith or for others; rather, a biblical love is expressed through our commitment to change our neighbor's condition. And we cannot do that without a personal spiritual transformation occurring in our own lives. (Jack A. Nelson, *Hunger for Justice: The Politics of Food and Faith*, p. 203; Orbis Books, 1980.)

This call of the gospel to love our neighbor as ourself may well provoke considerable anxiety, uneasiness, and stress within us. Indeed, unless we do experience some significant stress about the claims of the gospel upon our lives and our possessions, then perhaps we have not fully comprehended what it means to be Jesus' disciple. The record shows that Jesus' claim upon at least one person left the man with great stress when Jesus suggested that he sell all that he had and give to the poor. That young man went away sorrowful, "for he had great possessions" (Matt. 19:22).

Even just a casual reading of the New Testament will make it clear that Jesus did not offer his life just so you and I can live without any stress at all. One person made the observation that "Christ came to teach us how to be toward one another. You can't read the Bible and feel comfortable with ignoring what's happening in the world." And then that person went on to add:

> I think being a Christian puts a lot more pressure on you. I don't think Christ makes it easy for you to sit back and let it happen. You can't just say it's not your problem. Because Christ made it your problem!

Indeed, as ironic as it is, the fact remains that our efforts to live without stress, to live a life of ease without worry, as a rule lead to greater stress and worry for us. Recently, a couple with an annual income of over $100,000 was telling me about financial difficulties. One of their main problems is that they are constantly in debt because they have grown careless and irresponsible about managing their money. Likewise, numbing our brains with chemicals or spending to the limit of our credit is the way many of us think we can claim the good life, the trouble-free and stress-free life. And somewhere most of us know, too, that we are fooling ourselves!

"Take my yoke upon you, and learn from me" (Matt. 11:29a), Jesus still invites us. It is not an easy yoke in the terms you and I usually consider to be easy. But it does offer something more than the problems you and I bring upon ourselves when we think we are doing things the easy way.

Your Neighbor as Yourself

And loving one's neighbor as oneself is part of the challenge and the promise of that yoke. Moreover, with that promise is also the opportunity for us to trade some of our own problems for the larger problems of helping another person find food or shelter and live with just a bit more dignity.

The truth of the matter is that our baptism as Christians is, itself, a call to a life of service loving our neighbor as ourself. Many Christians are increasingly seeing that baptism is, therefore, a call to world citizenship. It is now plain in this small world we live in that the "good" Samaritan Jesus talked about is the person who walks down the roads that lead not only to Jericho but also to Harlem, and to Central America, and to Calcutta, and to the refugee camps that hold thousands of nameless, homeless, and starving human beings.

Gail Parker is typical of the growing number of persons who are feeling compelled by their Christian faith to invest more of their energy and resources in the needs of the world. She is a professional scientist and for many years has been quite concerned about the pollution of the environment. But the depth of her concern was dramatically broadened and deepened when she attended a national meeting of Presbyterian women a few years ago. During that meeting, her attention was constantly drawn to the theme of Jesus' ministry for aiding the poor, the captives, the blind, and the oppressed (Luke 4:18–19).

Meeting with so many other deeply committed and dedicated women, and seriously studying and meditating about the purpose of Jesus' ministry and the Christian faith, Gail realized that her whole outlook had undergone a transformation. She was persuaded that her former interests and concerns had been too narrow and that as a Christian she now had to be concerned about a broader range of issues. At that national meeting it had become unmistakably clear to her that widespread oppression is not God's picture for the world. Gail is convinced that "environmental concerns are still important, but matters of oppression, matters of injustice, matters of people being hungry in other places are important to me as a Christian, too."

Gail reports that she has become more involved by writing to her representative in Congress, adopting a simpler and less consumptive life-style, and speaking to her friends about issues of justice and hunger. She says that her friends have come to realize that part of the expression of her Christian faith is concern about the oppression of other people throughout the world. Now Gail says she has a different outlook about the sources of stress in her own life. "I have more stress if I'm only concerned about myself. Somehow there is a lot of release of stress for me that comes from doing things for other people . . . letting my voice be known on an issue that relates to oppression or hunger."

Like Gail, John Knight simply knows that it is essential for him to respond to human need. Commenting on his motivation for helping his church sponsor and bring a Vietnamese family to Minneapolis, he explained that "the Christian faith isn't what you say but what you do. That refugee family had a need, they were labeled 'hard to place,' so you do what you can to meet those needs." It is evident that for John and others like him there is nothing terribly new about extending love across cultures and across thousands of miles. For John it is simply a matter of living out the essential aspects of the Christian life.

Burnout and disillusionment are always the risk when we face the challenges of life and death to which the gospel calls each of us. However, in our struggle, we know that we are never alone. As one person put it, "I just keep reminding myself that it is really God's struggle for justice, and God is simply using my efforts." It is God's struggle, and we enter that service only on the grace of the strength which God promises to provide.

What Can You Do?

The following list of options for service as a world citizen is by no means intended to be exhaustive. Be creative as you join with others to ease the oppressive stresses and burdens felt by so many in our world.

1. Read Ronald J. Sider, ed., *Cry Justice: The Bible Speaks on Hunger and Poverty* (Paulist Press, 1980). This book is a compilation of countless biblical texts that deal with such subjects as God's special concern for the poor, economic relationships among the people of God, property and possessions, and God's concern for justice.
2. Participate in a covenant group for life-style assessment. Copies of the *Participant's Manual* for *A Covenant Group for Lifestyle Assessment* can be obtained from these denominational agencies:

    Presbyterian Church (U.S.A.), Church Education Services, 1101 Interchurch Center, 475 Riverside Drive, New York, N.Y. 10115

    United Church of Christ, World Hunger Action, 16th Floor, 475 Riverside Drive, New York, N.Y. 10115

    The United Methodist Church, Discipleship Resources, P.O. Box 189, 1908 Grand Avenue, Nashville, Tenn. 37202
3. Contact your member of Congress on key issues.
4. Give to your church's relief fund or agency.
5. Join a group of similarly concerned persons. Gather information from books, magazine articles, and newspapers. As a group, decide on action steps you can take to express your concerns and to influence public policy.

6. Talk with friends, neighbors, and work colleagues about your concerns without anger or self-righteousness.
7. Discuss the worldwide needs of others within your family circle. Let the supper menu, such as meatless meals, and the supper discussion inform the children that their parents are world citizens.
8. Write a letter to the editor on occasion. Know your facts and state your position convincingly.
9. Join an educational group within your church that can present informative classes and seminars for church members.
10. Pray for those who do not have enough; for those who lead; for the wisdom to see our own part in the problem; and for grace to take appropriate action.

(This list is drawn in part from Arthur Simon, *Bread for the World,* p. 144; Paulist Press and Wm. B. Eerdmans Publishing Co., 1975. This book is an excellent resource.)

Matthew Fox has emphasized that Christian compassion is not a matter of helping someone else's pain; instead, when you and I help another we are also helping ourselves. Compassion, in this world, is in everyone's best interests. "It is my pleasure," Fox says, "to be involved in the relief of the pain of others, a pain which is also my pain and is also God's pain." (Matthew Fox, *A Spirituality Named Compassion and the Healing of the Global Village, Humpty Dumpty and Us,* p. 33; Winston Press, 1979.)

Fox reflects Paul's own convictions about the stress and burnout faced by Christians in every age. We are called to share with others the same comfort we have received from God through Jesus Christ. "For as we share abundantly in Christ's sufferings, so through Christ we share abundantly in comfort too" (II Cor. 1:5). So this book on Christian renewal

Your Neighbor as Yourself

for living beyond burnout must close with that unexplainable mystery. Through Christ we are called to love, service, and suffering, and the mystery has always been that we continue to be renewed, renewed because we know how to love and take care of ourselves, and renewed because we give and share what we have in response to our neighbors' needs.

May God's compassion and grace always enable you to live beyond your own strength, and may you always be renewed by the opportunities for sharing that rich compassion and grace with your neighbor.

Questions for Thought and Discussion

1. How can affluent, privileged Christians justify their personal concern for stress management when most human beings in the world have basic concerns and needs for such life essentials as food, medicine, shelter, and relief from oppression?

2. What, in your view, are the main spiritual reasons that explain why most people find it so difficult to handle the stress in their life effectively?

3. What can your church do to educate and support persons to manage the stress in their lives more responsibly?

4. What are the distinctive characteristics of "the peace of God, which passes all understanding" (Phil. 4:7), and how can that peace help Christians cope with stress and burnout?

5. What are appropriate and effective ways for a Christian to intervene when a loved one or friend is showing signs of excessive stress or burnout?

6. How should a Christian view the relationship between spiritual or biblical resources and the insights of psychology and medicine for coping with stress?

7. What better goals for a fulfilling life does Christianity offer than the stressful and compulsive need always to be achieving so valued by our culture?

8. What effective strategies could a small group of Chris-

tians follow together that would show within six months that the participants were being renewed for living beyond their stress and were also living out their convictions to be world citizens in their concern for their neighbor?